Live, Grow & Be Free

A GUIDE TO SELF-PARENTING

Live, Grow & Be Free

DENNIS GIBSON

HERE'S LIFE PUBLISHERS, INC.
SAN BERNARDINO, CA 92402

LIVE, GROW AND BE FREE
A Guide to Self-Parenting
by Dennis L. Gibson

Published by
HERE'S LIFE PUBLISHERS, INC.
P. O. Box 1576
San Bernardino, CA 92402

Library of Congress Catalog Card 82-82412
ISBN 0-89840-030-9
HLP Product No. 95-039-4

For the sake of easier reading, the pronouns he, him and his in this publication refer for the most part to both male and female in the generic sense.

TABLE OF CONTENTS

Singleton

Gratis

10 March 08

76819

FOREWORD

Dennis Gibson says the familiar in novel and thought-provoking ways. When I read *Live, Grow and Be Free*, I was challenged to ponder things about myself which I knew already at an "in-depth level" but had tried to ignore. The author helped me to see myself more clearly and as a result I have grown.

Most readers will see themselves in this book. We all tend to be strong-willed, stubborn, guilt-ridden, unforgiving and self-centered at times. We treat ourselves like children and wonder why we remain spiritually and psychologically immature. Dr. Gibson helps us to understand this and guides us as we make growth-producing changes in our own lives. Creative illustrations, honest sharing from the author's own life, insight from his study of psychology, and truths from the Scriptures have been interwoven to produce an enlightening tapestry of helpful ideas for any person who wants life to be more fulfilling.

The book is provocative and in spots is controversial. Its author, an engineer who became a psychologist, is also clearly a Christian. *Live, Grow and Be Free* presents practical psychological insight to the non-psychologist Christian who is willing to look inward.

— Gary R. Collins

Acknowledgments

My deep appreciation to the Career Class at Wheaton Bible Church whose refreshing fellowship created an atmosphere in which I, as their teacher, gave birth to many of the thoughts contained in this book.

Thanks to my mother and father whose keen minds and passion for articulate speech my Heavenly Father used to kindle my love affair with language.

Gratitude to my wife, Ruth Flesvig Gibson, who preceded me in authorship and effervesced me out of introversion.

I owe to Wheaton College a debt I cannot repay — first, for midwifing me into the family of God as a thirteen-year-old in their northwoods Honey Rock Camp program; second, for breaking down a major portion of the prison bars of my own strong will as a thirty-nine-year-old child undergoing the Christ-orchestrated stress of a Wilderness Learning Seminar. Special thanks to the following wise agents of God's chastening love: Dave Russell, Harv Chrouser, Bud Williams, Mary Wetzel, and Lin Peterson.

My Encourager-of-the-Year award goes to Dave Enlow, former editor at Here's Life Publishers, for convincing me that someone might think I have something to write that is worth their reading.

Finally, I acknowledge how uplifting it was to hear Laure Rooker's laughter wafting in from her part of our office as she typed this manuscript.

D.G.

CHAPTER ONE

Control Is the Issue

I slammed my ski poles into the snow and glared at my feet. My right ski was crossed over my left, and I couldn't seem to untangle them.

This is ridiculous, I fumed. *These skis ought to do what I want them to do.* Furious, I scowled at my surroundings. I was alone in the north woods of Wisconsin on a wilderness seminar. My assignment was to use the cross-country skiing skills I had learned the day before to complete a seven-mile journey alone through the woods.

It *should* have been easy. I *wanted* it to be easy. To turn around this tree in front of me, all I had to do was move to the left, but I couldn't move my feet.

Seething, I panted as I struggled to make the skis comply. I punched the air with my fists and growled. My anger was like a child's tantrum, but there was no audience for me to impress. At whom, then, was I showing my rage.

I stopped to examine my anger. Maybe I'm mad at myself. But no, that was not the way I felt. I saw myself, rather, as an unfortunate victim, a sincere fellow simply trying to fulfill an assignment and have a little pleasure and comfort in life. I was incensed that someone or something wanted to deny me that.

Since there was no other human being within earshot, and I was angry at something or someone, there were only three possibilities left: 1) I was disgusted with my instructor back at camp for not having explained everything fully, not having taught me perfectly enough; 2) I was furious at the skis, the woods, the snow — in short, at reality for not cooperating with me, not bending to accommodate my will; 3) I was mad at God, the one person who is always present, and the one who is ultimately responsible for reality being the way it is.

But I was not mad at the instructor. I remembered what she said; I had no questions for her.

That left the other two options, which really merge into one. My wish to make reality conform itself to my demands was nothing less than striving for power equivalent to God's. I was setting myself in a position of rivalry with God. The way He had made things did not suit my convenience. He was the author of everything, and I was protesting the way He wrote the script. I am a grown man, but I was thinking like the strong-willed child I had once been.

I remember an event that happened when I was about four years old. I was a skinny, finicky eater, and my mother was determined to fatten me. She tried every way she could think of to get food into her first-born.

One night Mom prepared some homemade vegetable soup. She did everything to persuade me to eat it; she coaxed, she pleaded, she put alphabet noodles in it.

"Come on, please eat it, it'll be good for you. It's got all the vitamins and minerals that you need so you can run and jump and play." But her sales pitch did not register with me.

Suddenly she shifted tactics. "I will give you one more chance. Either eat the soup now, or I will take it away and you will have nothing to eat until morning."

I splashed my spoon once more. "No, I don't want it."

"Okay." Mom calmly took the bowl away. She had never done anything like that before, and I panicked.

"Wait a minute! I want it now. Bring it back!"

Mom quietly answered, "I'm sorry. You had your chance. You can eat again tomorrow."

What? Mom did not give in to my demand? She could resist my request for food? Had she forgotten that I was her emaciated, first-born wretch?

I said, "I mean it now. I really am hungry. I'll eat it."

"I'm sorry. You had your chance. Nothing until morning."

I escalated. "But I *need* it! I'm starving! I'll go *crazy* if I don't get something to eat!"

She began to waver. "You promise you'll eat it if I give it to you?"

"Oh yes!" I insisted. "I'll do anything! I promise I'll eat it!"

"Okay." She dished up the soup, and set it in front of me.

I looked at it and said, "I don't want that."

It was a power struggle, pure and simple. It didn't matter whether it was eating soup, or getting dressed, or leaving for school on time. The issue to me was how much I could control my mother. The prize was to make my will prevail over hers.

James Dobson's book, *The Strong-Willed Child*, guides parents and teachers to shape the will without breaking the spirit of a child. But what about the kids like me, whose parents never read the book? Or who read it and didn't follow it all the time? What becomes of the strong will in those children?

Since the will was never harnessed in childhood, it remains strong and undisciplined in the grown-up bodies of these imperfectly-raised human beings. And since none of us was ever raised perfectly in all aspects of our lives, we all have facets of our personalities that are not yet disciplined. We are all, then, to some degree, strong-willed adults.

The Bible gives us a prototype of strong-willed

behavior in the nation of Israel. The first chapter of
Deuteronomy summarizes a typical story. Moses said,
"Go up. Take the land."

They said, "No, we're scared."

Moses said, "O.K., you've lost your chance."

They said, "Oh, we were bad. Now we'll do it."
And they went up to conquer the land, against Moses'
stern forbidding. They met with disaster.

Such opposition is the main tendency in strong-
willed people of every age. Tell them cheerfully,
"Have a nice day!" and they'll say you're always trying
to boss them. They are allergic to orders. They even
sniff the pollen of commands when it isn't there —
then point themselves 180° in the other direction.

Strong-willed people have no alternative action or
policy to propose. They focus only on proving that
nobody can make them do anything they don't want to
do. By the time they reach adulthood, most people
have learned to camouflage their oppositional nature
with psychological and even physiological symptoms.

A man with a phobia in regard to airplanes, for
example, says he "can't" fly on business. For reasons
presently outside his awareness, he doesn't want to
fly, and he won't. His "can't" is less likely to draw flak
than is an outright "won't".

A woman frequently blows up at her husband and
children, saying she "can't" control her temper. She
means she *won't*. Evidence for that is her ability to
remain calm when guests visit.

"Can't" lives on "won't" street. But people who do
not want to accept the consequences for directly
refusing, camouflage their unwillingness with face-
saving excuses or even self-accusations. They learn to
trick others into believing it is not they who are saying
"I won't," but that their symptoms are saying it for
them.

A young Christian man says he is a terrible sinner

for his sexual promiscuity. What he means is, "I would rather blame myself than mend my ways."

An alcoholic anguishes in guilt over her drinking. It's as if she is striking a bargain: "If I punish myself sufficiently, I buy the right to continue drinking."

A husband "forgets" to call his wife to say he'll be late for dinner. He has promised her a hundred times that he will call. He arrives home late with another empty, "I'm sorry," another claim, "I feel so guilty," and another promise never to slip up again. We can translate his actions into the sentence, "I want you to think well of me even though I don't intend to change."

A man jumps off a bridge into an icy river to kill himself. A police boat pulls alongside to rescue him. He refuses to get into the boat, saying he is determined to die. A policeman pulls out a gun, points it at the man's head, and says, "You get into this boat or I'll blow your brains out!" The man promptly scrambles in.

Obviously the man's goal is not suicide, or he would welcome the officer's bullet. For him, the prize is not death, but control. What he wants is power — in this case the power to make other people regret that they had not treated him better while he was alive.

Other methods of opposition are more subtle. Shyness is an interesting way to refuse without appearing to refuse. Shy persons frequently prejudge how others will respond to what they offer. For example, the man who is shy about asking women for dates is saying in effect, "I know ahead of time that any woman I ask out is sure to reject my invitation. Therefore, I won't even give them a chance."

The person who holds back from contributing to a conversation and uses shyness as an excuse is indirectly telling others, "I know better than you do what value you will place on what I can offer. Since I

believe that you will react negatively to what I offer, I
am not willing to give you the opportunity."

Such self-protection is a sympathy-getting
smokescreen. It is basically a defensive refusal to carry
one's fair share of the load in social interaction. It isn't
that the shy person is *unable* to participate; the
problem is unwillingness. Shyness is more a symptom
than a problem.

Another symptom of a strong-willed nature is
being demanding. The central struggle of demanding
people is their insistence that they *must* have what
they *want*. They equalize "necessities" and "wants,"
and their "wants" become demands. Bill Gothard's
Seminar in Basic Youth Conflicts refers to these
demands as "rights," and popular terminology calls
them "needs." Psychotherapist Karen Horney (one of
the founders of the Association for the Advancement
of Psychoanalysis and the American Institute for
Psychoanalysis) identified them as "neurotic claims."

These are all names for the idea that because I have
done or been something virtuous, it is but a matter of
justice that things should go my way, and that nothing
adverse should happen to me.

The foundation of a demanding approach to life is a
series of false concepts:

(1) I've got to have what I want to have.

(2) What I want is the same as what's best for me.

(3) Love and approval from certain people (whom I
select) are absolutely essential to my well-being.

(4) When I do certain things just right, or suffer
greatly enough, I am entitled to something I want.

(5) If I blame, criticize, and punish myself, others
must overlook my wrongdoing.

Since it is a matter of "justice" and "should," the
strong-willed thinker becomes a self-appointed en-
forcer of these rules to keep them from being violated.

The main enforcement tool is the tantrum, which

comes in dazzling varieties. First, there is straight-forward intimidation by a loud voice from a red face. Common words hurled forth in these arm-twisting tirades include, "After all I've done... Who do you think you are...?"

Then there is the infamous silent treatment. When it bewilders target persons and they ask, "What are you mad about?" the punisher can spice up the sting of the silent venom by the hypodermic sentence, "If you don't know, I'm not going to tell you."

A third weapon is the pained expression. Its telephone equivalent is often used by strong-willed parents demanding exorbitant proofs of undying loyalty from their adult children. Some familiar martyr sentences are, "Well, I guess you don't love us anymore," or, "You'll never know how you hurt me when..."

Adults can expect such punishments from their strong-willed parents and parents-in-law when the adults set certain, appropriate limits, for example, on how many gifts may be lavished on the grandchildren.

Tears can be another powerful tool to enforce the demands of a strong-willed person. The excessive use of tears helps to create a pathetic picture of a fragile, buffeted soul who is entitled to demand of everyone else around, "Handle with care!"

Similarly, people-pleasing is a subtle way to demand that others please me! If I make myself a Pleaser, never asserting my own wishes, but always doing what I think you want me to do, I am really attaching a hidden string to my services. Since I try hard to please you, you must show that you are pleased with me.

Embarrassment is another particularly intricate way to demand attention. A blushing girl puts her hands over her face and squeals, "Don't look at me! I'm so embarrassed!" It's a disguised demand. Who can fail to notice the dramatic show she puts on? The only way we can be sure to follow her orders not to notice her blushing is to look closely to see if the tinge of pink is there, so that we know this is the time *not* to look at her. It is a paradox, equivalent to the command, "Do not read this sentence!"

Another tactic the strong-willed person uses to control his environment is complaining. By exercising muscles of self-pity, he builds his shoulders up and they become more adept at perennially bearing the crushing burdens of injustice. Consequently, the strong-willed adult becomes famous for his gripes. He is proud of his suffering, and his complaining reflects the attitude, "The world should see how much I put up with."

The language of protest often sounds like this: "Well, how would *you* like it if...?" But it really doesn't matter to the complainer how I would feel in the same situation. All he wants to hear is that I would be so uncomfortable I would endorse the attitudes and actions he shows. The complainer justifies himself with this unspoken idea: "If you fully realize how badly I am suffering, you *have* to agree with my conclusions."

There is a certain childish magical thinking behind complaining. The belief is, "If I appreciate what I already have, I won't get any more. Therefore, what I don't have is far more important to talk about than what I do have." One purpose of showing ingratitude, then, is to bid for bigger payoffs.

Sometimes complaining takes the form of quiet self-torture. An example is a man who continually reminds himself that his best friend and his ex-wife betrayed him. He thus achieves the following advantages:

(1)   He protects himself from his own vulnerability.

(2)   He justifies his own vengeful retaliations,

making them seem heroic, powerful, and impressive.

(3) He avoids the ordinary life task of grieving and getting on with his contribution to society.

(4) He beats to the punch anyone else who might fault him for having been stupid or blind or soft toward his wife and friend.

A strong-willed adult would rather continue to prove he got a raw deal than to put the experience behind him and get involved with the business of present living. He chooses to limit his growth now, because he did not get "X" in the past. Not only does this person prefer to remain socially dormant but the above processes are actually anti-social. Most people would say that a self-torturing man is being too hard on himself, and no doubt that is true. But he also is being hard on others. To the extent that he complains, he refrains from carrying his part of the load. The less he participates, for whatever reason, the more the rest of us have to do.

A cousin to complaining is belittling. "Belittle" is an interesting word for put-downs, sarcasm, criticism, ridicule — any maneuver by which one person seeks a superior position by making another appear inferior. It is literally a command: *"Be little,* so that I can feel big by comparison."

Similarly, sarcasm is a subtle way to put other persons into a one-down position. It is easily seen in the cutting comments high school kids fling at each other. It is a kind of jousting match, like verbal King-of-the-Mountain. A mixed message of humor and hostility, sarcasm is a brilliant barb that piggy-backs on a friendly gift and adds grit to humor. Like belittling, sarcasm enables the speaker to practice one-upmanship.

Strong-willed tendencies are expressed not only in psychological symptoms, but often they include physical distresses for which medical examinations reveal no physical cause. The list might include fatigue, headaches, colitis, and depression. Certainly these disabilities can be caused by medical conditions, but when they are not medically caused, there is still hope for sufferers. Psychotherapeutic treatment can help them to hear the eloquence of their own bodies which say, without words, "I don't want to do X, and I don't want to be punished for admitting it."

Whether they are physical or psychological, all strong-willed symptoms are characteristic of people who wander from the pasture of God's love. In his book, *A Shepherd Looks at Psalm 23*, Philip Keller tells of a wandering ewe who repeatedly left the richest pastures he provided for her. She stubbornly refused those and insisted on finding her own grazing lands, even though hers were always inferior to the ones he freely offered.

The prophet Isaiah compared strong-willed people to sheep:

"All of us like sheep have gone astray, Each of us has turned to his own way" (Isaiah 53:6, NASB).

The sheep-rebel turns down the shepherd's generous offer, complains that it's not good enough, and insists, "I'd rather have what I want than what is best for me."

But behind their belligerence, all symptoms of a strong-willed nature, all tools used to attain power, are S.O.S. signals. They are messages of distress which are broadcast to others in familiar patterns in order to protect one's self-esteem.

What lies behind this strange self-sabotage that interferes with a healthy self-image and damages relationships with others? Oddly, the answer lies in two desires basic to human identity: to *be* and to *belong*.

CHAPTER TWO

To Be and to Belong

*T*ake a coin out of your pocket. Notice that it has two sides, heads and tails. Now put it back into your pocket, and this time take out just the head side of the coin. You cannot do it; the two sides go together as one coin.

Just as you cannot separate the two sides of a coin, you cannot divide these two primary motivations in all human beings: to be and to belong. We all want to declare ourselves as individuals, and at the same time to be accepted by society. More precisely, we all want to know that we are a part of a particular group of persons.

Radio astronomers recently beamed a message into space, announcing that somebody is here on planet Earth. As intelligent beings, we want to know what we are part of. We want to know our place. In order to know if we *belong* to a universe of others, we have to declare our *being* here, available for relationship.

The coin of human personality calls for a unity of being and belonging, of initiating and responding. Only when others call for my response to their initiatives do I recognize that I am one among many. Only then can I experience the solidarity of belonging to a living entity larger than myself.

One of Satan's favorite lies is that we must sacrifice either our desire to belong in order to fulfill our potential, or we must abandon our identity if we are going to be a part of a relationship. The errors our parents made in disciplining us as children gave us the chance to believe Satan's lie.

Like all of us, our parents also displayed some of the strong-willed symptoms mentioned earlier. They refused, demanded, and complained — sometimes harshly, sometimes subtly. A cold shoulder, a turned-away face, the silent treatment, a scalding attack with knife-edge words — all these common forms of rejection taught us as children, "When you do what *you* want to do, you lose my love. When you do what *I* want you to do, you keep my love."

Of course, not everyone has experienced such harsh rejections, but it's probably safe to say that most of us have experienced them in varying degrees. To the extent we have, we mistakenly conclude, "Well, then, in order to be somebody, I must be an outsider. If I want to be accepted, I must be a nobody, with no ideas of my own, just a puppet who acts out the ideas of other, more powerful people."

Yet to isolate ourselves in the vain hope of finding ourselves is to divorce being from belonging. Since we want both to be and to belong, we soon learned as children to seesaw between the two positions. One time we would comply to be accepted, and another time defy, to be our own person. It's like shifting our hands quickly back and forth between the cold water and the hot water on a two-faucet sink, in order to come up with a blend of tolerably warm water.

With every repetition of the seesaw, we continually set more deeply into our subconscious beliefs the mistaken idea that to assert ourselves carries with it the price of being cut off and cast adrift from loving relationships. Since we have concluded that's how things are, we don't wait to see if our loved ones will cut us off; we act as if they already have. We become hostile toward them while we set ourselves forward. In the extreme, we act by the motto, "To live I must kill."

But Jesus said to live we must die. Die to what? Die

to the lie. Die to the seesaw. Die to our mistaken childhood beliefs. Die to our tendency to isolate ourselves to *be* ourselves.

"...unless a grain of wheat falls into the earth and dies, it remains by itself alone; but if it does, it bears much fruit" (John 12:24, NASB).

In order to become something newer, larger, more magnificent than I have been, I must be willing to leave behind what I am by myself, and participate in a process involving others. To fulfill my created potential, I must contribute to, identify with, and participate in an enterprise larger than myself. We call it mankind, society, the group; Jesus called it the Kingdom of God.

The grain of wheat multiplies and grows and produces food by ceasing to exist in its individual form. It gives itself to the earth, and the earth's forces act upon it to replace its original form with an enlarged outcome inherent within it.

But losing myself raises a question. What do I do about my self-esteem?

Today's humanistic psychology promotes the notion that you've got to love yourself before you can do anything worthwhile for anyone else, that you've got to look out for "number one." In this theology, "number one" refers to one's self.

But biblical theology speaks of *God* as number one: "...the Alpha and the Omega, the beginning and the end" (Revelation 21:6, NASB). Yet the one person in history who had the *right* to demand personal exaltation said, "I am not in search of honor for Myself — I do not seek and am not aiming for My own glory" (John 8:50, Amplified).

With that philosophy, Jesus passed the crucial test of mental health described in the early 1900's by Karen Horney and another famous psychologist, Alfred Adler. These two dissenters from Freudian psycho-

analysis said that the hallmark of neurosis is the
search for personal glory, honor, admiration and
superiority over others. Jesus left His exaltation in
God's hands.

The Bible and sound psychology agree that we all
tend to love ourselves too much already, and that the
way of life is to love our neighbors and ourselves as if
members of the same body. The apostle Paul gives a
prophetic list of strong-willed adult characteristics
that will abound in the last days. He begins the list
with, "People will be lovers of self" (2 Timothy 3:2,
Amplified). And today's literature in psychology and
psychiatry is rife with descriptions of the increasing
malady, narcissism.

Writing to a different audience, in a particularly
tender passage, Paul urges his beloved Philippian
Christians: "...let each regard the others as better
than and superior to himself — thinking more highly
of one another than you do of yourselves. Let each of
you esteem and look upon and be concerned for not
merely his own interests, but also each for the interests of others" (Philippians 2:3, 4, Amplified).

Paul does not urge his readers to love themselves;
he recognizes that they already do. Self-love is a
human tendency that he seeks to bring under
Christian discipline. In his letter to the Ephesians, he
says, "He who loves his wife loves himself"(5:28).
Note the order. Healthy self-love is a *by-product* of
going out in love toward others.

But the strong-willed adult has it all mixed up. He
loves himself in a self-centered, competitive way,
rather than in a self-sacrificing, cooperative way.
Interestingly, one example of self-centeredness is a
common mannerism that appears at first glance to be
self-sacrifice. It is false humility.

Suppose you compliment me and I reply, "Oh,
pshaw, I'm not really as good as you say." My negating

your statement is almost guaranteed to get you to give me more. It's an underhanded way of begging.

But beyond that, when I discount your appreciation, I am taking an arrogant stance. In effect I am saying to you, "I am a better judge of quality than you are." I dispute your judgment. It's as if we were standing together on a shore looking across the water at a flaming orange sunset. You, in breathless awe, say, "That is incredibly beautiful!" Then I frown and say, "Well, on a scale of one to ten, that's about a two."

When I throw away your compliments, I am saying in effect, "By my superior knowledge, I am able to render a more sophisticated assessment than you are." In true humility I could say, "Thank you very much. That means a lot to me."

We make ourselves vulnerable when we say, "Thank you." It's a simple, heartfelt human transaction, to let another person know, "You have deeply affected me in a way that I will not forget. I appreciate it."

But as a strong-willed adult I reason to myself, "If I accept your compliment I will be in your debt. And I dare not be in your debt, because you might exploit your advantage over me. And so I dare not let myself be vulnerable to you." What it boils down to is, by rejecting your compliment, I set myself up as your judge and critic. I am saying, "You are not trustworthy. You have impure motives, and I'll not let you affect me."

The issue is not my acceptance of me, by my unwillingness to be a part of *us.* It's my insistence on being different, special, separated out in a distinguished way. It's trying to *be* without also being willing to *belong.*

There is another human fascination that proves the strong-willed person has not too little love for self, but too much. It's revenge. I remember a war movie I saw as a child. Humphrey Bogart was with the good guys, guarding a water hole a desert. Bad-guy soldiers were out there trying to get to the water. The bad guys treacherously shot one of our guys who was carrying a white flag. The audience was incensed. Then Bogart angrily whipped out a machine gun and went "budda-budda," right down the line of the enemy soldiers — to the great satisfaction and cheers of all of us in the theater.

There is something in us that craves for the satisfaction of "getting back" at others who have hurt us. We seek revenge when we feel bruised at having been treated too lightly, having not been taken seriously enough, having been left out. The soldier who shot the guy with the white flag did not take seriously the sanctity of the truce. Identifying myself with the good guys, I felt he violated *me*, he wasn't taking *me* seriously, he wasn't treating *me* the way he should.

Revenge is a statement. If we put it into words, it goes something like this: "I am going to make you feel my influence. I am going to make an impact on you because I am worthy of your time and attention."

If our problem, then, is not poor self-esteem but powerful self-love, why do so many people have inferiority complexes? Isn't it possible to hate myself?

Let us say that my real self is what God made me to be. My real self is the image of God in me, including my capacity to change, grow, and improve. But my *idealized* self is an image of my own creation. This idealized image is striving, neurotic, vain, strong-willed, immature, competitive, undisciplined and childish. It seeks to outshine all other people.

Self-hate is the striving subject, "I," despising the real-self object, "me." We hate ourselves, not because we are worthless, but because we insist on being far more than what we are. We use self-blame to enforce the idealized self's "shoulds," which we view as the only path to glory.

We all have feelings of inferiority, that's just part of being imperfect. But healthy, realistic, mature people use their inferiority feelings as a mild incentive to grow and improve. The self-centering, strong-willed person regards inferiority feelings as a disaster. This intense preoccupation with one's own inferiority is what makes it a complex. People who focus narrowly on themselves do not attend to the needs of the society of which they are valuable members. They refuse to belong.

Hollywood movies appeal to inferiority complexes. They idealize the strong-willed adult who steps outside the rules, defies authority for a noble purpose, and prevails as an individual operating heroically in isolation from organized fellow human beings. The message that feeds strong-willed self-love is, "Success in overcoming inferiority comes by individual, deviant action, and contempt for rules and order. I am the authority around here, and everybody else benefits, because I, by my own definition, am good."

Much of the philosophy behind such a view stems from the advice, "Just be yourself." But the strong-willed person sees more in such a statement than, "Don't play roles and wear masks. Let people in on who you really are." Instead, the strong-willed lover of self takes the humanistic approach.

Humanistic wisdom says we must know our own minds and be guided by our gut feelings. Unknowingly, I tested that philosophy one day in the woods.

I pulled my jacket tighter against the chill as daylight began to diminish. The pine needles cracked under my hiking boots as I hurried nervously along. Night falls quickly in the woods, and I was lost.

My instincts told me my car should be off there to

my right. But I had been walking that direction for
some time already, and nothing looked familiar.

I glanced at my compass. It said the car should be
off to my left — exactly opposite of what *felt* correct to
me. Certain the compass must be wrong, I jiggled it. It
stayed steady.

I had to choose to go by what my feelings told me,
or by what the compass told me. The more I thought
the compass was correct, the more I stubbornly
wanted to go my own way instead. I wanted to be
right. I did not want to submit.

Finally, by an act of rational will, I decided to obey
the compass. I walked to the left and soon found my
car.

"He who leans on, trusts in, and is confident of his
own mind and heart is a (self-confident) fool, but he
who walks with skillful and godly wisdom shall be
delivered" (Proverbs 28:26, Amplified).

"There is a way which seems right to a man, but its
end is the way of death" (Proverbs 14:12). The strong-
willed child in me had been determined to go the way
that *seemed* right, in spite of great cost. For nearly a
mile I had been "true to myself," refusing to consider
any alternative.

But it's more than just a matter of "feelings vs.
facts." If I am a strong-willed adult, the humanistic
advice to "be yourself" is of no help to me, really. If I
were to just let go and be myself, I would destroy
anyone who ever gets in my way, including my
humanistic advisors. They imply by their advice that
they are willing to accept all my behavior. They would
quickly retract their counsel if I were to follow it.

They would replace their advice with something
more like, "Be kind to me, and find pleasure for
yourself in that." That advice comes much closer to
the biblical principle repeated again and again: "Love
one another." The ancient, godly wisdom recognized

that the only path to solid self-love is to direct love toward someone else. To be, I must belong. To belong, I must give of myself.

Surprisingly, the space race has made a discovery that suggests what one can do about inordinate self-love.

To reach Jupiter and the outer planets, a spacecraft from Earth must first slow down, drop out of its own orbit, and fall toward the sun. It must go the opposite direction in order to reach its destination. The sun's gravity then whips it into the far solar system.

So also we can only reach the deep space of proper love for self by going away from ourselves, first allowing ourselves to be pulled by God's love, then deliberately going out in love toward others. We must go the other way to get where we are headed. Thus we find our identity, who we are in the solar system of God's family.

Yet one aspect of our strong-willed nature interferes regularly with our ability to be and to belong. It is our powerful struggle to sit on God's throne.

CHAPTER THREE

The Right to Rule

I walked into my office one evening and hit the light switch. The lights didn't go on, though, and I became angry. I flipped the switch on and off several times — *hard.*

My action showed I believe in a power greater than my own: the electrical power supplied by our local electric company. I did not consider trying to illuminate the room by my own exertion. But at that moment, I insisted the power greater than I must operate upon my command. My anger said I would tolerate no defiance.

The Greeks called it *hubris.* We call it pride, conceit, vanity, arrogance. All of these imply an excessive estimate of our own worth, merit, or superiority. In the positive sense, our ability to be proud is part of our awareness that we make valuable contributions which enrich the lives of others. The humble baseball hero, Lou Gehrig, was proud to be a Yankee. He enjoyed using his God-given talents as a member of a team. He treasured what the other team members were able to add to what he gave.

But our wrongs are in our excesses. Our sin is not in using, but *ab*using, God's gifts — this interferes with our growth toward freedom. We start with a seed of something good, which God has delegated to us to use. Then we go beyond His intention and appropriate His gifts for purposes He never had in mind. Adding "ab" to the word "use" makes "*ab*use". The ab prefix means "away from." When we make too much of a good thing, we move away from God's purpose and it becomes a bad thing.

Strong will itself comes from God. Stubbornness is basically determination, the stuff of which first-century Christian martyrs were made. They *used* their determination to stay true to Christ as Lord; they did not *ab*use it by merely defying human authorities.

Atomic power is not necessarily bad. We can *use* it to generate electricity and to remove cancers. We can *ab*use this gift from God by making bombs to destroy cities. The strong-willed child in us is nuclear power not *yet* harnessed, not *yet* disciplined, not *yet* focused on constructive uses. It is renegade in us; not *bad*, just misdirected.

So, as strong-willed adults, we take the God-given ambition to become "partakers of the divine nature" (1 Peter 1:4) and inflate it into the satanic overambition to be "like the Most High" (Isaiah 14:14). We thus join the original rebel in a conspiracy of opposition against God's authority. There are no civilians in the cosmic conflict. We are recruits in one of two armies: God's by conscious choice, or Satan's by unconscious default.

To rebel is to hold the illusion of freedom. We think it's our own idea. It's not. It is merely our agreement to side with the age-old delusion that our remotest parents bought in the Garden of Eden: that it is *possible* for a human being to displace God and be kingpin (Genesis 3:5).

Satan tried to seduce Jesus with the same delusion. He threw three temptations at Jesus in the wilderness. The most powerful one went something like this: "Jesus, I will give You power over everyone else if You will be my slave. Just one little act of worship toward me and it's all Yours" (Matthew 4:8, 9).

The undisciplined strong-willed child in each of us faces that same temptation. We would love to have others under our power and control. That we can only be safe and content when we are finally able to force other people — and life itself — to conform to our will is a lie that appeals to us.

Striving for the throne is exhausting. Strong-willed adults long for relief. The path lies in acknowledging that the throne is already occupied. Yet even then, sometimes we insist that God be what we conjure Him to be, rather than seeking to discover what He *is*.

That's what the heathen do in idol worship. They create deities that are products of their own imaginations. Our idols are our declarations of how we see things to be. We then imbue those concretized perceptions with powers to function for our convenience. Yet they cannot truly function. Imagine a tribe of people living in a parched desert next to an artesian well. It would be absurd for those people to dig dry wells in the desert sand, and then pant for water by these dry wells, ignoring the clear, abundant waters of the nearby natural well. But Jeremiah 2:11-13 uses that picture to describe the Jewish people seeking satisfaction in gods that are not God. We can apply the same picture to ourselves. We seek approval, possessions, prestige and power, as if they were the Living Water for which our souls thirst.

Part of what we build into the gods we create is a bargaining orientation. We arrange to have them torment us, with the understanding that they are therefore in our debt and must exercise their powers for our benefit. We dictate the terms of the bargain. We even decide what sacrifice is adequate payment to appease this god and buy his favor.

There is a kernel of God's truth buried within idol worship: power over me does rest outside myself. But the God of the Bible takes initiative out of man's hands. *He* offers the sacrifice. *He* defines and refuses

to be defined. *He* calls Himself "I am." *He* demands
the price from *us*.

   Nearly a hundred years ago, Hudson Taylor wrote:
How few of the Lord's people have practically
recognized the truth that Christ is either "Lord of
all" or He is "not Lord at all!" If we can judge
God's Word, instead of being judged by it, if we
can give God as much or as little as we like, then
we are lords and He the indebted one, to be
grateful for our dole and obliged by our compliance with His wishes. If on the other hand He
is Lord, let us treat Him as such. "Why call ye me,
Lord, Lord, and do not do the things which I say?"

   What God asks of us is obedience, which Bill
Gothard defines as "yielding the right to have the final
decision." Yet we stand in contempt of court. We not
only break God's laws; we also oppose His right to
rule, demanding it for ourselves. The trouble is, we
only hurt ourselves when we insist on being our own
boss.

   Jesus ran into just that kind of self-demanding
rebellion one day in Nazareth. The people there were
offended by His wisdom and His authority, and they
refused to cooperate with Him. "And He could do no
miracle there except that He laid His hands upon a few
sick people and healed them" (Mark 6:5, NASB).

   Jesus was rendered powerless to do miracles
without cooperation from His needy neighbors. By
their unbelief, His hometown friends had handcuffed
the God of the universe. He has created us as
decisional beings, who can choose to stunt our
relationships. He also has created us as relational
beings; we can flourish only by cooperating with His
initiatives.

   Cooperation, obedience, submission — whatever
name one attaches to this quality God asks of us —
behind it lies an even stronger motivation: trust. Yet

the strong-willed adult is plagued by lack of faith. This need to trust can be illustrated by something that happened to me one day in the woods.

I stopped for a moment and surveyed the forest around me. The air had that freshly-washed fragrance that invites you to breathe deeply, and I complied. I'd entered a small clearing, and this looked like a good place for a brief rest.

Just ahead of me were a couple of trees. I could lean against one and catch my breath. One stately old tree seemed especially inviting, but then I spotted another one that appeared to be stronger. As I leaned against it, a crackling noise startled me. Suddenly I was sprawled on the ground, the dead, rotten tree beneath me.

I got up, walked over to the other tree and pushed cautiously on it. Satisfied that it was sturdy and could be trusted, I leaned against it. It held, and my trust increased: the tree would support my weight.

Early in the twentieth century, Alexander Souter wrote a resounding definition of faith. He said faith is "the leaning of the entire human personality on God in Christ Jesus in absolute trust and confidence in His power, wisdom, and goodness."

So then, to lean our personalities on God is to say that we *know* He is solid and strong. Yet often we reveal a different attitude. By refusing to trust God with our whole personalities, we act as if God is unsound wood that cannot support us.

Where do we get the information that God is *not* firm? Nothing authoritative about God describes Him that way. The Bible calls Him a rock, absolutely solid, dependable, faithful, trustworthy. What authority are we consulting when we then conclude that God is not reliable?

The answer is we are setting *ourselves* up as the authority we will follow. As strong-willed adults who are not trusting God, we are taking the attitude, "I

know more about God's character than anybody else
does. I am far more committed to my own well-being
than God will ever be."

What we believe in our hearts, revealed by our
actions, contradicts what we believe in our heads,
revealed by our words. We deify our feelings. We go by
what *seems* right to us. We choose against the external authority of God's word. In so doing, we are
contesting one or more of these three attributes of
God: His power, His wisdom, and His goodness.

Suppose I am in a situation that threatens my
security, and I feel great anxiety. I know in my head
that the Bible tells me in Philippians 4:6 not to be
anxious about anything, but calmly and confidently,
with thanksgiving, make my requests known to God.
But suppose I persist as a strong-willed adult in
fretting over my situation, and not uttering a single
thankful word to God.

If I am doubting God's power, what I am saying to
myself is, "My circumstances are bigger than God." J.
B. Phillips wrote about this in a book called *Your god
Is Too Small* (1961). The error in doubting God's
power is in considering Him small and weak. This is
"97-pound weakling" theology. Philosophers used to
debate whether God can create a rock too big for Him
to move. In my doubt I say, "Yes. My circumstances
are a rock too big for God to move. Since God is great
and powerful, this probably does not happen with
other people, but my case is different."

Sometimes it is not God's power that I am doubting, but His wisdom. Then I am thinking, "My circumstances are unknown to God. He just doesn't
realize what I'm going through. If He knew, He would
certainly do something to relieve me, since He is
mighty enough and loving enough. But, alas, the great
God of the universe, Who is interested in the lilies and
the locusts, knows nothing about *me.*" This is the

theology of the low-I.Q. God. Maybe J. B. Phillips should write a second book: *Your God is Too Dumb.*

Other times I doubt God's goodness. My line of unconscious reasoning is, "My circumstances don't matter to God. The God who so loved the world that He gave His only begotten Son callously refuses to give me the simple solution to my problem." This theology casts God as the unmovable iceberg. Mr. Phillips also could write *Your god Is Too Cold.*

All three show the insolence of doubt, and doubting God is arrogant. "My circumstances are too tough. God doesn't realize what I am suffering. God cares about others but not about me." We tend to see ourselves as broken, bruised, and all out of gas. But we do this in such a way as to make God, the heavenly Father, appear to be guilty of child abuse! By our loud suffering, we are reproaching God. We are proclaiming Him to the world as a cosmic bully.

Seldom would any of us say out loud that God has failed us. But we are eloquent by our downcast countenances, and by the conspicuous absence of praise from our language. Our unspoken attitude is, "God has ceased to be dependable. He has singled me out for special abuse. The Almighty drops whatever else He is doing in remote parts of the universe and devotes His time and attention to making *me* miserable."

Self-pity is self-piety. It is a neurotic tendency to which we are all prone, and in which the strong-willed adult specializes. We are the object of our own worship. We seek for identity and distinction by suffering. We wallow in lack of faith. We actively keep it alive.

Actually, we seldom question God's power or wisdom. That is evident in the way we whine at Him in our prayers, "Why did this have to happen to *me!*" Because God has all the resources and knowledge to remedy what is happening to us, our "why" is not really a question, but a protest. We don't want an answer but an apology! We are insisting that God ought not to have let this horror fall upon us. We claim special exemption from this kind of affliction. And we require that God *must* do something about it since He *can.* We end up suspecting that God has not answered our prayer because He is not really good.

Doubting God's goodness probably grows out of our experiences early in life. God allowed us to learn of His nature from imperfect representations of Him. What an amazing risk God has taken by entrusting His reputation to how mothers and fathers represent Him!

Many parents, lacking maturity, try to build their own self-esteem by humiliating their children. They make unkind comments like, "Oh, that's crazy! You could never build that!" Or, "What? You want to be a doctor? Why don't you just learn your math first, you dummy?" Children from that kind of background might think God is unkind because He — like those imperfect parents — needs to make Himself feel bigger by making us feel smaller.

Or, we might conclude that God has ceased to be good because He is basically selfish. Maybe we had experiences with parents who put themselves first. They might have set their own convenience ahead of their responsibility to care for us. They may have missed the outstanding privilege of making upstanding adults of their strong-willed children.

We also may have decided that God is not good because He is indifferent. We might believe, "He doesn't even care enough about me to pick on me. He is bored with me. He yawns when my name comes before Him." That attitude could come from childhood experiences with mothers and fathers who protected themselves from the demands of parenthood, at which they were afraid they might fail. They may have been fearfully looking back over their shoulders at the imperfect authorities who criticized them when they were young.

So goes the curse of the generations, "...to the third and fourth generations of those who hate Me" (Deuteronomy 5:9). We are all in that chain somewhere.

We are all shortchanged compared to what we wanted as children and what would have been nice to have. But those of us who complain about being shortchanged reveal something about our thinking. We expect the link ahead of us in the chain to be perfectly intact! Other parents may be imperfect, but we think our moms and dads owe it to us to be psychologically whole. We consider it our birthright! And our parents look around, bewildered, asking, "Hey, wait a minute. Why am I supposed to be so healthy? Nobody ever showed me how."

Unfortunately, parents are handicapped, especially toward their first-born children. They have never done this child-raising before. They do not know how to recognize perfectly what their offspring are hungry for. A lot of them are still starving from what they didn't get from *their* parents.

We have all been victimized in some ways by the unloving chapters in our ancestry, so we, too, tend to pass on our parents' inaccurate conclusions about God's attributes, in addition to those conclusions we have formulated for ourselves.

We tend to assume, like spoiled children, that God loves us only when He gives us what we expect and want. We overlook the fact that, since He created us, He knows better than we do what is best for us. Our strong-willed contrary attitude is, "If it's not what I was looking for, it's not what I ought to have."

But true faith is not anticipating *what* God will provide, but *that* He will provide abundantly for us beyond what we ask or think. Little-faith people limit themselves to their own imaginations of what they would enjoy.

Jesus understood this, and so He used exaggeration to convey how very eager God is to lavish His favor upon us. In Luke 11, Jesus says in effect, "Look, you people are familiar with how even an unrighteous person will finally give in to the nagging of someone who asks a favor. Therefore, if even self-centered persons will grant the request of someone whom they resent, your Father, God, who loves you tenderly, will respond to your persistent praying. You don't have to twist God's arm. He is eager to prosper you."

But we think, "Aha, you see. The power is in the nagging. If I can irritate God badly enough, I am more likely to get what I want than if I merely trust His good will." Doubting God's willingness to be good to us, we take matters into our own hands. We place more confidence in our ability to pester than in God's likelihood to be generous, and we apply this erroneous thinking to other relationships as well.

We thus choose to alienate ourselves. We decide that the only way to get the favors we want is through extortion. By irritating others enough, we can make them grant us what we want as a payment to get rid of us. We decide we are willing to pay the price, to lose the relationship in order to have the power to get our way.

That is why Hebrews 11:6 says that without faith it is impossible to please God. We cannot have a friendly relationship with someone when we are putting distance between that person and us. To try to manage God by pestering Him is the opposite of trusting, appreciative interaction with Him. Faith says, "I am willing to be related to and ruled by You." Distrust says, "I prefer my lonely dictatorship over a friendship with You."

The strong-willed adult fights being under God's

power, thinking, "If I accept any gift from You, God, I will be one-down. I will be opening the floodgates to a barrage of Your domination and control. And You are sure to abuse me if I allow You such power. You will be no more kind to me than my parents were when I submitted myself to them." Another, more bitter view of God as a bad parent says, "If I accept something from You, I will by my action be telling the world that You have done right by me. And I refuse to give You that satisfaction."

The truth is that I belong in society and in the universe because God has created me and assigned to me a place of His design. My task is to take my place and to do fully what He has equipped me to do. Yet I insist on making my own way so that my place and my security will be under *my* control. I am taking over the creator's job. Displacing the Most High. Usurping the right to rule.

The Scripture squarely confronts this strong-willed rebellion. The apostle Paul tells us that through faith, we become forever secure in a "place" of loving relationship to God, the author of all relationships. It is definitely "not of works, lest any man should boast" (Ephesians 2:9). It comes by God's generosity, which we can appropriate only by our trusting, cooperative response.

God's way is a step at a time. The request in the Lord's Prayer is for our daily bread; God does not equip our digestive systems to handle one magnificent meal that will last us the rest of our lives. Like the manna He provided daily for Israel in the wilderness, His deal with us is, "Take what I offer today, and trust me to know best and to provide what you will need for tomorrow."

When I jog around our neighborhood, I feel so tired in my chest and legs that I usually think I cannot make it to the end of my run. But wherever I am, no

matter how tired, I am confident I can take one more
step. Maybe that's what the Bible means when it says
we *walk* by faith.

The process of my running, not the far-off finish
line, becomes my focus. Faith is not feeling, but
movement, action — like my step-by-step process of
running. It is acting on my confidence that I can take
the next, single step. Faith is my continuing, my
enduring, my persisting. What is it we seek, then?
Perhaps we can get a clue from Paul, who spoke of
striving like a runner: "I press on to lay hold of... that
[let us call it "X"] for which Christ Jesus... laid hold of
me" (Philippians 3:12, Amplified).

"X" must be a very compelling, desirable goal
indeed. It must be one for which a sensible person
would be willing to pay a high price. It must be similar
to what Jesus was after when, for the joy that was set
before Him, He endured the cross, despising the
shame (Hebrews 12:2). Imagine that! Something
meant enough to Jesus that He willingly endured all
that we abhor most passionately: pain, rejection,
ridicule and death.

What was that "joy that was set before Him"? What
is our "X" according to Christ? The next phrase in
Hebrews 12:2 tells us that Jesus has sat down at the
right hand of the throne of God. There it is! You see,
we seek *most* deeply not the throne, but a place with
the one who is already on the throne! We confess with
St. Augustine, "Thou hast made us for Thyself and our
hearts are restless til they find their rest in Thee."

How, then, did we start striving for the throne in
the first place? Why are we at war with ourselves and
with God? And what can we do about it?

CHAPTER FOUR

Roots and Mental Maps

*F*our-year-old Stanley overheard his parents discussing his father's forthcoming fishing trip. "I want to go, too, Daddy!"

"No, son," his father replied. "Not this time." This could have been a simple event in which Stan learned to take no for an answer. But three people made too big a deal of Stan's deprivation.

Stan inflated the episode by throwing a tantrum. He bellowed a protest from his wounded want.

"I said *no!*" growled Father. "You're too young. You'll never be able to sit quietly in the boat."

"Yes, I will. I'll be quiet," Stan howled.

"No, you won't! You'll be loud and wiggly and you'll scare the fish away. You can't go!" Father was shouting by now, adding fuel to the fire because of his anger.

The more Dad berated Stan's qualifications, the more Stan felt justified in crying, "Foul!"

Mother complicated the matter further by feeling sorry for Stan. Peeved at Dad, she unwittingly reinforced Stanley's immature belief that an angry no from Dad was far too difficult a burden for him to bear.

"That's not fair," she told Father. "You're acting like one little boy can ruin your whole day! It wouldn't kill you to take him with you. There, now, Stanley. Mommy understands," she soothed.

She implied agreement with her son's notion that he was being treated most unfairly, and therefore that he was entitled to punish the world by sulking. Years later, when Stanley had become an adult, he still brandished the weapon his mother helped him learn: self-pity.

Dad could have taken Stan fishing. It might have been a fine investment in their rapport and in Stan's healthy self-esteem. But Stanley need not have learned self-pity even if his father denied his wish. The raw materials for self-pity were some out-of-proportion reactions.

First, Dad overdid the way he turned down Stanley's request to go fishing. He took a bland, ordinary event and colored it red by his anger. He marked it in Stanley's mind that being told no is really an extraordinary incident.

Then, Stanley portrayed Dad's actions as cruel and unusual punishment. He magnified a happening into a holocaust. He nominated himself for Victim of the Year.

Finally, Mom seconded the motion, and encouraged Stan's self-pity. Scowling at Dad and looking with forlorn, furrowed brow upon fragile, battered Stanley, she in effect validated her son's notion that he needed what he wanted. She fed his feeling that if he did not get what he had a right to demand, a gross injustice had indeed been inflicted upon him by a harsh and uncaring authority.

That early family climate was ideally suited for Stanley to develop an angry style of relating to others. He saw it work for Dad. He equated anger with power and concluded that those in authority use their size and that irresistible power of anger to make others weak, little and manageable. The only hope little people had was to grow big and angrily intimidate others. Dad showed anger to Stan. Mom showed anger to Dad. Stan impressed Mom by his angry tantrums. Little wonder Stan's wife complained thirty years later that Stanley regularly became irritable toward her when things were not going his way.

The core of Stanley's strong-willed adult mentality is his conviction that he can force life to meet him on his terms. Like all children, he was influenced by the decisions and behavior of his parents. The self-pity they inadvertently nourished limited the development of freedom in his life and seriously impaired his potential.

Children, like young scientists, experiment with different ploys, to see which ones other people will allow to work. One example is the helpless ploy. It works with certain people who get their sense of dignity and importance from being helpful. A basically sociable attitude like helpfulness can become antisocial when inflated out of proportion. For one person to be help-*full*, requires that someone else be help-*less*.

A typical example of the inadequacy ploy occurred when Sharon, age 5, dawdled in trying to tie her shoelaces. "I can't get it right," she whined in a tone carefully beamed in to Mother's wave-length. Mother responded indulgently with, "Oh, here. Let Mommy do it for you, Sweetie."

What appears on the surface to be compassion is really Mother's vote of no confidence in Sharon's ability. Mother's overdone servanthood promotes in Sharon's mind the unfortunate belief that ordinary tasks are far too difficult for her to master. This is particularly hazardous if Sharon is unusually pretty. She might get much more attention for being cute than for being capable. When Mother takes Sharon's charm as an acceptable substitute for competent action, she is training her daughter to act helpless. Then the girl grows up strong-willed and handicapped.

There is a common variation on the above "compassionate indulgence" theme. Suppose Mom reacts to Sharon's whining by nagging, "Oh, go ahead and do it yourself. Can't you see I'm busy?" Then

Sharon dawdles some more, escalating from helpless to brainless: "Which lace do you put on top?" With that, Mom exasperatedly says, "Oh, never mind. I'll do it, dummy. I swear, sometimes I wonder if you'll ever amount to anything."

The humiliation Sharon suffers in the second instance is, in her mind, a small price to pay for the powerful position of making Mom do her bidding. In both examples she learns that she can *make* Mom tie her shoes. She can make Mom her slave. The same helpless gambit can appeal to Mom's pity or Mom's impatience. Either way, Mom has taught Sharon to use her strong will to put others into her service. She has inadvertently schooled her daughter in incompetence.

In their book *Children: the Challenge*, Rudolf Dreikurs and Vicki Soltz cite several examples of parents who patronize their children. One tells of a child who had been seriously ill and long afterward could tyrannize Mom into servile obedience by sobbing, "How can you be so mean to me when I've been so sick?" Another mother vowed never to cross her daughter, because the poor thing had been born out of wedlock, and Mom wanted to make it up to her.

These examples show that parents sometimes take offense at hardships that have come upon their children. They are bitter toward fate, life, reality, circumstances — ultimately toward God. Their attitude is that God has unfairly allowed this child to suffer, and that He should have known the child was entitled to better treatment. Out of spite toward God, they try to do better than He did, to right the wrong. The child by contagion picks up the same spiteful attitude, in the sense of "the world owes me."

while our parents, our childhood families, and ur culture influence us, they do not determine ly decisions we make in life. We all have our own style. My style of relating to others may be similar to that of my sister, but it will not be identical.

Before we reach the age of ten, we all make decisions by which we shape our basic personality structures and which, together with parental influences, form our psychological roots. In these decisions we invest certain goals (like being right, pleasing others, or getting high grades) with energy that makes them like electromagnets to us. These goals become treasures toward which we move. We say to ourselves, "If I can just attain *that*, I will be OK" (meaning accepted, adored, safe, invulnerable to humiliation).

That inner sentence is a statement of faith! By it we confess a lie as if it were the truth. Our early decisions to empower certain goals to magnetize us actually authorize Satan to work in our thoughts, emotions, and actions. We activate created things to be greater treasures to us than the Creator Himself. "Where your treasure is, there will your heart be also" (Matthew 6:21 KJV).

While we are making these decisions and establishing our psychological roots, we are also exploring and settling the new world of life outside the womb. So, we all make mental maps early in life, telling us what the world is like and where we are in relation to other people and things. Unfortunately, our mental maps are like the delicate and yellowing one I saw recently on a souvenir shop's wall.

Explorers in the early 1700's had drawn this intriguing map of the Great Lakes region. In those days, cartographers had partial, imperfect information about shorelines and river locations, and consequently the map was severely inaccurate. Yet the mapmakers did the best they could. Those early explorers and settlers were certainly better off with a poor map than with no map at all.

So it is with each of us. We need some way to make sense of what we experience. Just as rivers, lakes, mountains and deserts are illustrated on a paper map, our mental maps consist of beliefs, philosophies, concepts, impressions, ideas, views, conclusions and theories. Yet because we base them on incomplete information, our mental maps are as distorted as that one on the souvenir shop's wall.

Paper maps can be inaccurate in two principal dimensions: longitude and latitude. Mental maps can err in the two dimensions of being and belonging. People often deviate on the "being" axis by believing the necessity notion: "In order to be anybody, I've *got* to have what I want to have." On the "belonging" axis, they often adhere to the heresy of entitlement: "I have a *right* to be loved, approved, and accepted by certain other persons I select."

Topographical maps indicate elevation along with north, south, east, and west. You can even find them sculptured in three dimensions, to show mountains and valleys. In our childish mental geography, we greatly magnify the matter of elevation. We emphasize who is up, who is down; who is above whom, and where do I fit. It's as if our physical stature relative to grown-ups becomes for us a parable of our worth. To be big is to be powerful and worth much. To be small is to be weak and worth little.

We experience disappointments and feel inferior, as if we are in a valley, compared to the mountain peaks we aspire to occupy. We want to rise, not just to level ground, but to the heights — not just to adequacy, but to superiority. We so overemphasize the up/down dimension that we diminish our attention to north/south, and east/west. How severely we thus limit our own freedom of movement! We deprive ourselves of the contentment of living on the level with our fellow man.

As children we were particularly concerned about finding a place. A mature adult view sees "place" as a vantage point from which to contribute to society. To a still-undisciplined child's mind, "place" implies a position of prestige society owes him or her.

Bigotry is a seriously childish belief that generates such hostile statements as, "They ought to know their place." By this the bigot means, "These other people are below me in intrinsic worth. They ought to show it by deferential actions and by granting me the priority to have things function for *my* convenience more than for theirs."

It's as though we recognize that Pike's Peak and Death Valley are two different wonders to behold, but that we wrongly say that Pike's Peak is better because it's higher. Jesus attacked the mistake of comparing on a scale of value when He exposed this common elevation exaggeration in a story he told.

An employer hired a number of farm hands to labor in his fields under the hot sun for many hours. They agreed on a fair contract for a full day's wage. Later that same day, he hired another group of men, saying he would pay them fairly. These worked only one hour instead of the full day that the first ones worked, but the employer generously paid them all the same.

The first group argued that they should have received more than the newcomers. Their standard of fair pay was not what they had contracted for with the employer, but what *other* people were getting. They mistakenly compared their money not with what *they* had the day before, but with what others received. Here is the heart of jealousy: comparing our fortunes with the fortunes of others. It is a self-defeating action.

Why do some people persist in such baffling behavior? Perhaps the motto, "The prize is worth the price" can help us understand.

Let's say that a woman we'll call Louise demands unqualified, constant approval from her loved ones. In this case, the prize is predictability. Louise is willing to pay the price of painful rejection in order to prove that her mental map works. When Louise finally receives a blast of annoyance from her badgered husband, she is able to say, "See, my map was right! Any time I try to ascend the Mountain of Approval, others put me down into the Valley of Rejection." A common, irrational conclusion resulting from that belief is, "Therefore, I've got to redouble my efforts to get people to approve of me."

Louise was not entirely incorrect. It is true that her efforts to manipulate others only caused them to be upset with her. It is not true that being more manipulative will help the situation.

Heresies are seldom totally false; rather, they are truths out of balance. They are half-truths we enlarge into mockeries of the whole truth. There really is a Green Bay off the western edge of Lake Michigan. But, on the early French explorer's map, Green Bay appears as big as Lake Michigan! Truth out of proportion is not as aptly called "untrue" as it is "misleading." That is the key point about our childhood mental maps; they mislead us in our adult walk.

Basically out of an unbalanced diet of nurture and admonition, not suited to the needs of our particular inborn temperaments, as children we developed grotesque irregularities in our mental maps. In a nutshell, our psychological cartography developed like this:

(1) As newcomers to the human landscape, we were impressionable and needed to make sense of life.

(2) Our parents followed the best maps they could find, but because those maps were archaic, our parents made mistakes in raising us.

(3) We distorted what we saw, through lenses

warped by the stresses put upon us by those mistakes.

(4) We set for ourselves an idealized self as our goal, and charted a course to get there. The journey was never possible because the destination was a Shangri-La existing nowhere in reality, but only on our mental map.

(5) Though we did the best we knew how under the circumstances, we could not avoid coming to mistaken conclusions.

(6) We are all living by archaic mental maps which are products of our own participation in the fallen human condition. These maps are ours to do with as we choose. We can regard them as the finest finished products possible for us ever to achieve, or we can view them as working rough drafts for improved later editions.

Strong-willed adults have love affairs with their first mental maps. They act like proud Great Lakes tourists who buy the map on the souvenir shop wall, and then drive according to it, saying, "If it was good enough for Pere Marquette, it's good enough for me!"

But here is some good news: the map is not the territory! No map can ever duplicate exactly the ground it symbolizes. Since we cannot carry an acre of real estate in a pocket, we make models of it that are small enough for us to use. That means we have to scale down from reality to representation. Therefore, no map can ever be anything but a distortion. We can no longer refer to maps as "true", but as "relatively useful" for the journey we have in mind.

Even the best mental maps by which mature adults live are distortions of reality. The task in making mature maps from childish charts is to reduce big mistakes into little ones. Twentieth-century maps *more nearly* represent the Great Lakes than did the primitive ones two hundred years ago. We are less likely to get lost following an up-to-date map than if we limited ourselves to one from long ago.

Yet our old maps are not utterly worthless. They do enable us to get around reasonably well. It's just that there's more available to us than we allow ourselves when we stick slavishly to obsolete editions. They can serve as starting points for improved maps! Everything we can do following an old map we can do less painfully with a new one.

Now as a strong-willed adult, I would rather bully reality into bending itself to fit my theory than revise my theory to fit reality. Why? Because to revise my theory would be to admit it was wrong or imperfect. That would reflect on me as an inadequate, inferior person — an image of myself which I will not tolerate.

What a burden to fight reality. Jesus said to Saul of Tarsus, a strong-willed adult, "It is hard for you to kick against the goads" (Acts 26:14, NASB). And Jesus said that His burden, the yoke of reality, is light by comparison to our self-imposed tonnage. What a relief to regard my original theory not as "wrong", but as "partially true, and capable of being expanded in the future"!

So, I face an internal struggle. On the one hand, as a strong-willed adult, I want to follow my old, familiar map. On the other hand, as a mature, reasonable adult, I want to develop a better one. Where did this dichotomy originate — and what can I do about it?

CHAPTER FIVE

Choosing the Real Me

W hen we leave childhood and move into adulthood, we all acquire the responsibility to
finish the work that Mom and Dad started in our lives.
We all become parents to ourselves. The bad thing
about that is that we are very likely to continue our
parents' mistakes against ourselves. We are too per-
missive with ourselves in some ways, too harsh and
critical in others. Consequently, the sins of one
generation pass on to the next, and so on.

To understand how the chain of generations affects
us — and how we can break it — let us examine the
psychological theory of human personality taught in
transactional analysis. This theory uses everyday
terms readily understood by non-psychologists, and it
has been popularized in such books as *Games People
Play* by Eric Berne, *I'm OK — You're OK* by Thomas A.
Harris, and *Born to Win* by Muriel James and Dorothy
Jongeward.

One especially useful feature of this theory is that
the personality can be illustrated in diagrams as well
as in words.

In this approach, the three principal parts of one
personality are called Parent, Adult, and Child
(capitalized to distinguish them from persons who
might be parents, adults, or children). Each of these
parts can be represented as a circle. The three stacked
upon each other then make a snowman picture of
human personality, as shown in Figure 1.

The Child is the foundation of the structure of
personality. It contains our innate desires for self-

expression and relationship with others. The Child is the "feeling" and "wanting" dimension in each of us. It is the seat of our dual motivation to be and to belong.

The Adult is the rational, thinking aspect in each of us. Like a computer, it is objective.

The Parent is a collection of rules, guidelines, principles, shoulds and oughts that each of us carries around. We picked most of these up from our parents when we were little, hence the term Parent. One

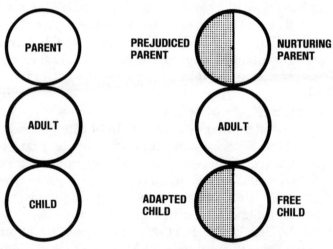

FIGURE 1 — Simple Snowman
Structure of Personality.

FIGURE 2 — Elaborated
Structure of Personality.

might think of the Parent as an internalized authority figure — a portable Mommy or Daddy, if you please.

We can further divide the Parent and Child into two sides, much like the old and new natures in Christian doctrine (See Figure 2).

The top snowball in Figure 2, the Parent, has both a bright and a dark side. The negative side, on the left, is the Prejudiced Parent, whose influence stifles, disheartens, cripples and inhibits the Child. The Prejudiced Parent is the source of internal accusations such as, "You'll never amount to anything." "Why are you such a sissy?" and "If only you had been a boy."

The positive side is the Nurturing Parent, nicely typified by the father who waited for his prodigal son to come home. He loved both his sons, and was utterly devoted to their good, even at considerable inconvenience to himself. Jesus related that parable to illustrate the nature of God the Father.

The Nurturing Parent is the source of internal assurances, for instance, "I will never leave you nor forsake you." "I love you the way you are." "I love you too much to let you stay the way you are." and "Be good to yourself." Note that loving discipline is a function of the Nurturing Parent because it promotes the growth and well-being of the Child.

The Child within us can either be child*ish* or child*like*.

One day, Jesus took a little child on His lap. He turned to His disciples and said, in effect, "If you want to enter the Kingdom of Heaven, you must become *like* this little child" (Matthew 18:3). Why? Because heaven is a sandbox! The main activity there is playful, intimate joy.

In Figure 2, the positive, child*like* side of the personality is to the right. It is called the Natural or Free Child. This is the spontaneous, curious, life-loving, uniquely individual core of each person's personality. The main characteristics of the Free Child are joy, enthusiasm, honest grief with unrestrained tears, creativity, awe, intimate lovemaking, and exploration. This is the child-*like* image of God in each of us — the real self. God is creative, playful, trusting, tender-hearted, life-loving. Those are the qualities we most enjoy and admire in children.

But there are also child*ish* qualities within each of us. These are the undisciplined aspects of our lives, the qualities embraced in the term "strong-willed child." The childish aspects are what the apostle Paul refers to as the old nature in us, in contrast to the new nature that is recreated, child*like*, in God's image.

In Figure 2, the dark, negative, child*ish* side of the personality is to the left. It is called the Adapted Child. Note the past tense, reflecting a completed adaption to a former, threatening, interpersonal situation. The Adult is the only adap*tive* part of the personality.

The Adapted Child is a rebel against authority, in open defiance or in resentful compliance. Characteristics of the Adapted Child are types of behavior used to manipulate others: temper tantrums, procrastination, whining, pleas of helplessness, and anything else that would fit a scriptural definition of sin. This type of conduct indicates the strong-willed child is still present in grown-up persons.

The two natures wage war within us. Our old, child*ish* nature isolates us, promoting our individuality at the cost of our commonality. This child*ish* nature in the strong-willed adult disputes God's right to exercise final authority.

On the other hand, the new, child*like* nature in the disciplined and mature adult delights in God's authority. It enables us to participate with our fellow man and find our individuality as we contribute to the common good. Figure 3 shows the original Parent-Adult-Child snowman separated into two halves representing the two natures.

The old nature consists of Prejudiced Parent and Adapted Child locked in a power struggle, like a bad father and his disobedient son. This clash goes on outside Adult awareness, because of the barriers that both sides erect against thinking, which is a mature, Adult function. We continue as adults to do *within* ourselves what we used to do as children *between* ourselves and grown-ups.

The Prejudiced Parent is like a self-centered mother or father who uses his power over the Child for

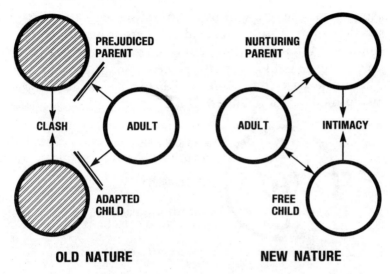

FIGURE 3 — *The Old and New Natures in a Christian's Personality.*

his *own* advantage and convenience, not for the well-being of the Child. He is a figure of selfishness. He never earns the respect and obedience of the Child.

Neither does he set an example of obedience, because he is not responsive to any authority higher than himself. He has never grown up, because he has never consciously resolved the authority question in his own life by an Adult choice to obey God-ordained authorities. By default, the authority whom the Prejudiced Parent serves and represents is Satan. And Satan fools him into thinking that self is in control.

The Prejudiced Parent is not really a person, but more like a memory or a composite photograph of big people who influenced each of us as youngsters. Therefore, the childish character of any person's Prejudiced Parent consists of the strong-willed child traits ingrained in the big people who raised that person. Consequently, the Prejudiced Parent consists of Child, Adult, and Parent parts (See Figure 4).

As Figure 4 illustrates, the Parent and Adult

aspects of the grown-ups who influenced the personality blend into the Prejudiced Parent but they are shadowy. What is active, interestingly, is the grown-up's irresponsible, undisciplined Adapted Child. That's the part that Mom and Dad used when they disciplined Junior in anger.

FIGURE 4 — The Prejudiced Parent in the Old Nature.

The Adapted Child is never secure. He realizes that he would not know what to do with his power if he won the struggle with his Prejudiced Parent. He knows he needs to depend upon someone stronger, older, and wiser than himself. His dilemma is that he dare not depend on the only Parent he knows about, because that Parent is not trustworthy. Therefore, the Adapted Child uses clever antics to manipulate the Prejudiced Parent into serving him on the Child's terms. These antics often include psychosomatic symptoms, helplessness, depression, and anger.

For example, the Adapted Child pleads helplessness by pouting over a difficult project and whining, "I can't do it." The Prejudiced Parent finally gives up in exasperation, and utters some internally inspired reproach such as, "Well, if you're too lazy to do it, you might as well quit. If you weren't going to finish it, you never should have started it in the first place."

The Adapted Child thus succeeds in getting parental permission to quit. All that's necessary is to play helpless and endure the pain of a curse (the label of "lazy" and implied worthlessness). That pain is the negative emotion that accompanies any manipulative symptom. It is the price which the Adapted Child insists on paying to gain the prize of Prejudiced Parent permission.

The old nature in each of us therefore consists of two self-centered agents at war with each other, and ready to do battle with anyone else who threatens to take control. Each agent claims the position of highest authority in his or her own life, and imagines that every other person does the same. Surrender, submission, obedience — these are unthinkable. They constitute humiliating defeats.

In his letter to the Ephesians, the apostle Paul clearly states his view that the way we live is the result of our choices. Just like taking off an old garment and putting on a new one, we can make Adult choices to activate either our old nature or our new nature.

"Strip yourselves of your former nature — put off and discard your old unrenewed self — which characterized your previous manner of life and becomes corrupt through lusts and desires that spring from delusion; and be constantly renewed in the spirit of your mind — having a fresh mental and spiritual attitude; and put on the new nature (the regenerate self) created in God's image (Godlike) in true righteousness and holiness. Therefore, rejecting all falsity and done now with it, let every one express the truth with his neighbor, for we are all parts of one body, and members one of another" (Ephesians 4:22-25, Amplified).

What is this new nature, that Paul asks us to put on? When we make the choices necessary to activate our new nature, what will happen? How is this reflected in the human personality?

The new nature in any Christian is an integrated personality that includes Nurturing Parent concern, responsible Adult thought, and Free Child enthusiasm (See Figure 3). The Adult adds an element of flexibility not found in the irrational old nature. Scripture reflects this openness in God. He invites, "Come now, and let us reason together, says the Lord" (Isaiah 1:18, NASB).

The mature character of any person's Nurturing Parent consists of the cohesive functioning of all personality dimensions in the grown-ups who raised the person. The Parent and Adult components within the Prejudiced Parent were drawn shadowy in Figure 4, to indicate their nonfunctional presence. By contrast, Figure 5 depicts the full, functioning presence of all three aspects of Christ's personality in the Nurturing Parent portion of a Christian's new nature.

**RESPECT FOR
AUTHORITY AND JUSTICE**

REASONABLENESS

PLAYFULNESS, TENDERNESS

FIGURE 5 — The Nurturing Parent in the New Nature.

The Nurturing Parent is like a godly father who cares for his daughter or son unselfishly. He cherishes life and uses his power to provide for the Free Child's protection and nourishment. He has grown up. He's resolved the authority question by choosing to obey the Author of life, thus ending the tyranny of Child desires.

He therefore sets for the Free Child (or real self) an example of joyful, thinking respect for the authority of government, employers, parents, and God. Like a good father or mother, the Nurturing Parent is a model of self-discipline and godliness. He disciplines for the Child's well-being, even sacrificing his comfort and his own life if necessary.

Yet the Nurturing Parent respects the Free Child's occasional testing of the limits. Sometimes the parent responds to limit-testing by enforcing the limit with firm discipline and explaining why: that the Free Child must rely on the Parent's judgment in setting rules for the Child's protection.

The good Parent shows respect for the Child by the act of consistently responding to the limit-testing. That is the opposite of discounting. The good Parent says by these responses, "What you do counts with me." The parent need not approve the new limit requested by the Child. If that were the only response the Parent ever made, the Child would really be the one in authority.

The Free Child is like the obedient daughter of a godly father. She feels secure because she has decided that the father is trustworthy. She responds joyfully to discipline because it lets her know the limits within which she is free to explore, grow and express herself without danger. The Free Child knows that to follow the wishes of the Nurturing Parent is not to give up well-being. The Child willingly goes in the path shown, and excitedly shares the goals of the Nurturing Parent. Both believe that life is good. They are siblings, in a way, both exulting in God as their common Father.

When I am jogging, I feel like I'm going to die. My Free Child feels disheartened when I think of the distance yet to be run.

My Nurturing Parent, not a slavedriver, says, "You don't have to push yourself. Your health is more important than finishing any race. So if the pain gets too much for you to handle, just stop and walk awhile and resume jogging when you can. How about it? Can

you take one more step? Or do you want to stop now?"
My Free Child answers, "No, I can take one more
step. In fact, I can make it to that driveway up there."
My Nurturing Parent says, "OK, that's fine! Don't
push yourself too hard. Just do what you can do."
So then, my Free Child can trust my Nurturing
Parent not to require more of me than is possible for
me, and at the same time encourage me to do what I'm
capable of doing. This is the way the Nurturing Parent
in me earns my respect, by accepting me as I am.
Either to demand that I do what is beyond me, or to
discount my ability to do what is possible for me,
would be to reject me.

In a way, my jogging is a parable of walking in the
Spirit. God does not require of me a commitment to
run the whole race of life at once. Walking in the Spirit
means that living a godly life is done one step at a
time, one driveway at a time. Nonetheless, it is a
matter of choice.

Fifteen hundred years before Paul and Jesus, an old
man stood in the dust of a desert, addressing the entire
people of Israel. In this, Moses' last conference with
the people, he struggled to summarize his entire
teaching. The book of Deuteronomy is his sermon.
Repeatedly, he punctuated his message with the
statement, "I have set before you life and death...So
choose life in order that you may live" (Deuteronomy
30:19, NASB). The theme of choice is a dominant
challenge in the Bible.

The same choice faces us: to remain strong-willed
children all our lives is the way of death; but to honor
God as the ultimate authority is the way of life. He is
the raw material from which we are made.

How, then, do we make the necessary changes in
order to bring our wills under the authority of God?
How can we change ourselves? Where do we find that
life in which we are finally free to grow?

CHAPTER SIX

Freedom Through Surrender

*E*very few years an article appears about some Japanese soldier, on a remote island in the Pacific Ocean, who is still fighting World War II. He learns that Japan was defeated, but when he goes home, he also learns that his nation really "sort of" won the war, considering the great prosperity she now enjoys. That heritage then becomes his as he lays down his arms. Surrender frees him from the bondage of battle. He was a fugitive only as long as *he* kept the war going.

That same principle is true in our relationships with others and with God. As we cooperate with Him, we free ourselves from bondage to our strong-willed self-determination. This happens when we surrender to the freedom He has made available to us.

A young man named Gary learned this principle through counseling.

From as far back as he could remember, Gary had heard his parents say "Gary's going to be a doctor, just like his father." That was the last thing Gary wanted to do, since his parents had pushed it down his throat. Yet his interests were most keen along the lines of medicine. When he took high school aptitude tests, the results showed he was highly qualified and motivated for a medical career.

When he entered college and had to choose a major, Gary was determined not to pick pre-medicine. A counselor helped him to see that he was making himself a prisoner. Defying his parents' wishes gave him an illusion of freedom. At the same time, it blinded him to the fact that he was enslaving himself in his own rebellion. By his strong-willed logic, he couldn't do what he wanted to do, if his parents also wanted him to do it.

"To be an individual," he reasoned unconsciously, "I must *not* do what Mom and Dad tell me to do." He ruled out a large area of freedom for himself, by holding on to the notion that to go into medicine would be to give in to Mom and Dad and be their little puppet.

The counselor suggested a way for Gary to step out of the prison of his own thinking. With a twinkle in his eye, Gary went home to his parents and said, "Folks, I want you to know I have decided to go to medical school, even though you want me to."

It was a simple change in wording, from "because" to "even though" his parents wanted him to. He had been stuck on a point of pride when he thought there was no way for him to become a doctor without it looking like he was doing so *because* his parents commanded him to.

It was as if God had beckoned Gary to an adult level by saying something like this:"Okay, Gary. Your mom and dad have finished their job with you. Their wishes are now irrelevant to *your* choices. *I* have something in mind for you to do. In fact, I even knew what I was doing in all those events that you thought were blunders back there in your childhood. I assigned you to the particular parents I did to groom you for a particular use I have in mind. I know you don't like my methods, but I can live with that. I designed you to enjoy serving Me as a doctor. Now let's get on with it."

All our qualities come ultimately from God. He gives them to us to use in His program of wooing the world to Himself. He is looking for recruits. He created each of us able to choose whether to join Him or jilt Him. He makes us able to respond, that's the meaning of "responsible." We can respond "Yes" to His invitation, and use His gifts in His service, or we can say "No," and abuse His gifts for our own, self-centered purposes.

For us to choose God's will has to be a choice we make, even if our parents want us to. "I have decided, Mom and Dad, that I am going to be a committed Christian, and attend the church you attend, even though that is what you have been nagging me all these years to do." That responsible declaration of independence could free many young adult and teenage rebels from the prison of pride into the delight of discipleship.

Choose this day whom you will serve. You are not serving Mom and Dad when you decide to go to *their* church on *His* orders. It is not capitulation to Mom and Dad, but surrender to Almighty God. It is an act of worship — of responding to God's love.

Our hardness to God's love-call indicates what worth *we* place on *God*. Note what placing worth on God means. It means worship — attributing worth-ship to Him. The choice we make is to decide whether God is worth more, or whether He is worth less, than the substitutes for Him that we have discovered.

The choice we make about God's worth to us has much to do with what kind of parent we assume Him to be. We take our distorted, prejudiced views of ungodly human authority figures and mistakenly make those our picture of God. This is a process psychologists refer to as "transference." We transfer our opinions and feelings about one authority figure to another, as if the two were identical persons. Our doubts about God's power, wisdom and goodness represent just such a case of mistaken identity. It is a mistake we need not continue to make if we acquaint ourselves more deeply and thoroughly with God's worth-ship.

How can we know who God really is and what He is really like? One way is to begin to identify the

mistaken concepts we have about Him, concepts that
have misguided our thinking until now. One of God's
characteristics about which we most often confuse
ourselves is discipline.

When we do something contrary to God's laws,
how does it affect Him? Our mistaken idea of God
assumes that our offenses *annoy* Him. Scripture
teaches that they *grieve* Him (Ephesians 4:30). Grief
implies that He is painfully afflicted by the temporary
loss of a cherished fellowship, which we have broken
by our misdeed.

We are taught in 1 John 1:9 that, no matter what
we do, God is faithful and just in His response to us.
He is true to His own nature and promises. That is,
God Himself adheres to a pre-set standard. He does not
deal with us according to His whim or His momentary
convenience, or His irritation with what we have
done. He is faithful to something that He has, in a
sense, made higher than Himself: His word, His
promise, His salvation covenant with us.

This covenant has two phases. The first is the
transaction in which we accept God's gracious offer of
a place in His family. We agree to be His children and
to live under His authority. That contract is un-
breakable. It becomes the secure fence within which
we romp and exercise. It is an overarching umbrella,
larger than any event that takes place under it.

This umbrella-like contract allows us then to enter
into the second phase of the covenant, the process of
being refined and disciplined. Here is where we kick
and scream and disobey, and God disciplines us. We
have an understanding that He is never to take us
seriously when we say we don't want the relationship
with Him. We are free to have our tantrums because
the umbrella, the container created by phase one, is
secure. We are in God's family by phase one. We are

groomed continually into being respectable family members by phase two.

Jesus showed what kind of parent He found in the one He called Father. His view is reflected in the father-like offer He made to those who considered following Him: "Take my yoke upon you...for my yoke is wholesome (useful, good) — not harsh, hard, sharp, or pressing, but comfortable, gracious and pleasant; and my burden is light and easy to be borne" (Matthew 11:29, 30, Amplified).

The Master struck a correct psychological balance between no discipline or harsh discipline, between spoiling or supressing a child. Both of these lead to inferiority feelings against which children stiffen their strong wills long into adulthood. But Jesus compliments His children by entrusting them with meaningful work to do (a yoke), and making sure that it is well within their ability to do it.

The feelings of failure and inferiority which we experience with the mind of Christ are different from those we experience with the mind of self. We see them not as disasters, nor as God having given up on us, but we see them as loving spanks from our Heavenly Father, Who says, "I see much that you are able to do. I have a place and a use in mind for you. I invested part of Myself in you when I created you. I made you capable of more than you have already attained."

The sour, negative, strong-willed child in me tends to look upon the place set for me and resent it. "This is your place," to a rebel's ears means that some self-centered authority has ordained for me a rigid, frozen location where I *must* sit. The eyes of my new nature see that my place is one of many possible places my Father makes freely available to me. My outlook is a matter of how I read His intentions. My old nature is sure that the authority wants to bind, restrict, trap

and imprison me. With my new nature, I know my
Father wants to welcome, provide for, enjoy, nourish,
and bring pleasure to me.

The nurture *and* admonition of the Lord are
necessary to civilize a human child. Nurture develops
the "be"; admonition develops the "belong."

With nurture alone, I could develop the mistaken
idea that I am the *only* person who is important. I may
conclude that I am the only initiator, and that all
other persons exist merely to respond to me. I would
then view my will as supreme, and have no question
but that I am the rightful dictator of the universe.

With admonition alone, I could mistakenly
conclude that only other people are important. I may
decide that the only way for me to be somebody is to
annoy all those other important people. Better a
nuisance than a nobody. Too much emphasis on
belonging may stir in me the belief that others do not
consider me capable of having anything to contribute
from my own creativity.

So, God balances nurture and admonition. His
discipline is like that of a coach who makes an athlete
strain to develop the full potential of each muscle. Go
out to any athletic practice ground — football,
basketball, whatever it is — and you will hear the
players complaining, "Oh, coach, can't we quit a little
earlier today?" The coach says, "Two more laps." At
that moment, the players *hate* it. They say, "It's not
fair! This guy is not human! He's brutal!" But when
the season is over, they say, "Boy, I'm glad he never let
us off easy!" They are glad because they have
developed.

In Hebrews 12 the writer speaks tenderly of God as
a Father chastening us. The writer knows how
chastening can affect each of us because he says, "No
discipline at the time seems pleasant." But in the long
run, when we recognize the loving hand behind the

pain, when we see the growth that we have experienced, we praise Him.

The great devotional writer, Oswald Chambers, once wrote that we are often more interested in God's blessings than in God Himself. We are thus like self-centered children on Christmas morning, who ravenously open our gifts, loving them more than we do the giver. What goes through the mind of a loving father thus ignored and treated like a vending machine?

He is concerned for the child and creatively plans how to jolt or maneuver the child's distorted thinking into a desirable, appreciative, and cooperative relationship. Similarly, God engineers natural consequences into our experiences with life, so that we come to know His thinking behind the order of creation. It is the same cooperative *relationship* with which He has always been concerned.

Here is a somewhat different view of Christ's sacrifice from that which we usually consider. Christ died not so much to benefit persons, as to benefit the *relationship* of those persons with God. In 1 Peter 3:18, we read that He died that He might bring us to God. He is like a matchmaker, wedding us to our Maker. Not just coincidentally, this verse comes right after instructions to husbands concerning their marital responsibilities.

Christ did not die so that we could live *instead* of Him, but so that we could live *with* Him. The former, mistaken idea is something like, "There's only room for one of us in the lifeboat, so I'll let you live while I drown." Neither partner in any relationship is to become a nobody so that the other can be a somebody. Both are to invest their somebodyness in a radiant relationship.

To say a person has worth or value is to formulate half a sentence. It begs two questions and raises a

third: Worth what? To whom? Who says? These
questions reveal a search for a source, a valuer, an
authority behind the action of attaching worth. This
quest implies our awareness of a person larger than us,
who initiates relationships with us.

Our parents were the original super-human in
whose eyes we wanted to be worth much. Now as
adults, when we feel worth*less*, we ache with the
dangling half-question, "Do I have any value?" We
used to seek evidence from Mom and Dad of our
importance to them. Though we no longer look to
them as our source, we have not yet identified a new
one. We are stuck with the unanswered questions of
our half-sentences. We wistfully yearn for some
authority to come along and fill those gaps that our
parents left.

The Christian message emphatically completes
the half-sentence. What are we worth? To whom?
"God so greatly loved and dearly prized the world that
He [even] gave up His only begotten Son, so that
whoever believes in (trusts, clings to, relies on) Him
may not perish — come to destruction, be lost — but
have eternal (everlasting) life" (John 3:16, Amplified).

As reassuring as the above words sound, they do
not always quench our desperate thirst for a sense of
personal significance. Why? Maybe because we have
two electromagnets near us, each capable of attracting
and holding us. Jesus alluded to them in this
penetrating admonition to the most stubborn, strong-
willed adults He faced, the scribes and Pharisees:
"...for the sake of your tradition (the rules handed
down by your forefathers), you have set aside the Word
of God — depriving it of force and authority and
making it of no effect" (Matthew 15:16, Amplified).

It's as if Jesus is telling us that we have two
switches at our fingertips. One sends current to the
Word-of-God magnet, the other to the human-heritage

magnet. By our will, we choose which magnet to empower. When we are not soothed by the words of God's love in John 3:16, it's a sure sign that we are somehow choosing to switch energy into the nonsense we began believing early in life as mistaken participants in a world of deluded thinkers.

Near the end of his life, John wrote his first letter. An old man with great wisdom, he cautioned his readers: "Little children, keep yourselves from idols — false gods, [from anything and everything that would occupy the place in your heart due to God, from any sort of substitution for Him that would take first place in your life]" (1 John 5:21, Amplified).

We are little children. And we need to root ourselves in the only valid authority, the God Whom John heard Jesus call "Father." Therefore, the cure to our own emptiness is to magnify His fullness. The more we deliberately value His greatness, the more we feel the compliment of His valuing us. Self-worth is a by-product of worshipping God.

CHAPTER SEVEN

Mind Renewing

*T*he streets were filled with people from every country — Mesopotamia, Judea, Rome, Libya, Egypt. Jewish people from all over the world had crowded into Jerusalem to celebrate Pentecost, the Feast of Weeks.

Peter stood outside and addressed the crowd, explaining the death and resurrection of Jesus. When they heard his sermon, the people were broken-hearted. They pleaded with Peter to tell them what they should do to change the sinful condition he had exposed in them.

He told them to repent, to change their views. He also told them to be baptized, to take a specific action consistent with their new views (Acts 2:38). This passage reveals two realities.

First, our views and intentions are directly under our power and ability to choose. We are responsible for our attitudes and motivations. Otherwise, the command, "Repent!" would be impossible, absurd, and unfair.

Second, the new attitudes and actions we deliberately choose are to reflect the authority of Christ over us. That is the meaning of being baptized "in Jesus' name."

How, then, do we change our minds and our behavior? Paul showed us one way to handle the dilemma when he said, "And be not conformed to this world: but be ye transformed by the renewing of your mind, that ye may prove what is the good, and acceptable, and perfect will of God (Romans 12:2, KJV).

Romans 12:2 teaches that we change our living by
changing our thinking. The simplest changes we can
make are in the labels we attach to the events in our
lives. We can use our negative feelings as windows
into our souls. We can look in, or listen in, and detect
what names we must be calling things in order to feel
toward them as we do. Then we can consider what
other labels could apply. We can dramatically change
our feelings toward a person, thing or event by
selecting a positive label from the list.

What are you looking at right now? Is it a book?
Paper and ink? Black and white? English words?
Written language? Chapter Seven?

Which of these terms is the one correct, true label
to attach to what is in front of you? That's right! No
single one alone is *the* true label — *all* are correct. The
name you select to represent what you are reading
depends on what purpose you have in mind.

It is the same way with the circumstances we face
in life. We can call each one by several valid names.
We choose labels that help us to accomplish our goals.
The labels we choose determine how we feel and what
we do.

A perfectionistic student who insists on getting
straight "A's" on every school assignment might think
of a "B" on an exam as "cruel and unusual punishment." The resulting mood is easy to predict:
irritation, depression, brooding, thoughts of telling off
the teacher, ideas of quitting school altogether, or
maybe savagely increased determination to stay up
later and study harder and never again to allow such
an unthinkable disaster to occur.

That student could create much more manageable
feelings by regarding the "B" as "a mild disap-
pointment, an inconvenience, a tolerably unpleasant
outcome," or even as "above average performance."

Persisting in positively relabeling my wife's words,

actions and intentions does much to protect our marriage from the ravages of my strong-willed tendencies. I'm super-sensitive to having a fault pointed out in me. One day my wife, Ruth, told me I had dominated a conversation we had with a friend, and that I had not given our friend a chance to say what was on her mind.

My first impulse was to defend myself, but I deliberately held back and quickly prayed silently, "Thank you, God, for allowing Ruth to mention this to me. Is there something here You want me to learn?" After a second or two, I realized that I agreed with her. I took what was for me a giant step forward and deliberately said, "I think you're right."

In my mind at that point I had done all that anyone could reasonably expect of me. I had gone the second, third and fourth mile with Ruth, and expected her to say "OK" and drop the subject.

Instead, she continued, "Yes, I think I am right because Martha needed a chance to talk. She was all bottled up with feelings, and you weren't giving her a chance to express them."

That statement from Ruth, even though she said it calmly and kindly, was painful for me. I felt humiliated and burned.

But this is a pattern between Ruth and me that we have discussed and about which I am gradually changing my mind. So, this time I did not retaliate with anger like I had done in the past, always to Ruth's bewilderment. I realize that her intention, in continuing to talk after I've said that I agree, is not to singe me. In fact, it has almost nothing to do with me.

My ancient error has been to assume that Ruth was demanding some response from me after I said, "I agree." She does not demand or even want a response from me. I *imagine* she wants me to crawl on my hands and knees, confess that I am wicked and terrible, and vow I'll never do it again. She doesn't want that. She just wants to put *her* thoughts together. If anything, all she wants from me is permission to assemble her thoughts, say them, and be relieved. Maybe at most she'd like a grunt from me or perhaps, "I'm with you, Honey."

So, like conversions to Christ, sometimes our mind-renewals are instantaneous, as was the switch Gary, the medical student, made from "because" to "even though." Other times it's gradual, like a child growing up in a Christian home, or like my deliberate, year-after-year changing of my perception of Ruth's intentions when she continues to talk about my misdeeds after I have agreed that they are misdeeds.

The key to positive relabeling is to recognize the positive intention that is behind what other people say and do.

One husband was furious at his wife for her frequent comments, grimaces, and groans about his driving. He regarded her actions as "criticism." Using that label, he made *himself* mad at her as he worked himself into feeling small and resentful. He searched for another label for her actions and came up with "request." She was simply making a request that he slow down, allow more space behind the car ahead, and come to stops more gradually. These he could easily do. Thinking of himself as "granting my wife's requests" gave him a feeling of masculine magnanimity.

Strong-willed adults generally cling to the notion that criticism directed at them is an unthinkably dreadful assault, one for them to ward off and neutralize by severe counterattacks against the critic. But in John 18:23 Jesus vividly showed us a realistic adult's attitude toward criticism.

Having just been punched and rebuked for not answering the high priest's illegal question, Jesus responded with the following attitudes: (a) If I was wrong, please point out My wrong; cite the godly principle I have violated. (b) If I was not evil or mistaken in what I said, I am curious about your motivation in punishing Me. I call you to consider what is motivating you, what your goals and purposes and standards might be, and what authority you obey, and who or what your god is.

We can adopt similar attitudes toward criticism. We can challenge our old notion that it is a blow to our self-esteem and use it as information about ourselves from which we can benefit, or as information about others with which we can confront them for their benefit.

We can also use the same approach to self-criticism. When I see with the eyes of my new nature, I fall short of my godly ambitions every time I look through the old goggles of gloom. But what I call these shortcomings is now altogether different. They are no longer "failures," but "opportunities to learn." Inferiority feelings are not crushing curses, but valuable information on places I have yet to grow. They let me know what muscles Coach God is seeking to develop in me, so that I can be increasingly useful to Him.

A young man — we'll call him Jim — worked in public relations with a Christian agency. He was overly concerned with approval. When he sensed people might react unfavorably toward him, he could hardly think of anything else. His inordinate "need" for commendation was interfering with his efficiency at work.

Then he began to use his imagination in connection with Paul's words to young Timothy: "Do your best to present yourself to God as one approved, a workman who does not need to be ashamed and who correctly handles the word of truth" (2 Timothy 2:15, NIV).

Jim began to attach a whole new meaning to the word "approved." He visualized himself as an unashamed workman standing before God. He saw God give him a sword (the Word of Truth), and commission him to go forth in radiant Government Issue uniform (the mark of approval in God's Kingdom), swinging that sword as necessary in the King's service.

"Approved" now meant for him "selected and sent" by God, at God's initiative, not Jim's! He wept with relief from the burden of having to earn acceptance again and again. He experienced more fully, in his inward being, the meaning of that familiar Scripture that says salvation is a gift from God, not of works, lest any man should boast (Ephesians 2:8, 9).

Recent neuropsychological research on the brain suggests that its two halves specialize in complementary functions. One side controls the process of logic, reasoning, calculating, using language — what we experience as conscious and voluntary. The other side controls our more nearly unconscious functions of visualizing, dreaming, feeling, making stories, producing artistic creations.

In most of our efforts to change, we hammer away with the verbal, logical side, trying to talk ourselves into behaving as we should. We can greatly aid that process by adding to our logical audio some brilliant video from the other side of the brain. In so doing, we are literally getting our head together. We can create experiences in our imagination that have as powerful an effect upon our subsequent attitudes and emotions as any past experiences that have happened to us. Ruth Carter Stapleton refers to this technique of inner-child healing as "faith-imagination."

We can modify the word "imagination" slightly to make it "image-in-action," or mental movies. Note how near to the heart of God our creative visualizing

must be. Since He created us in His image, for us to
create images in our minds is a personal way to
imitate Him. This is supremely characteristic of
beloved children! They constantly try to do things like
their fathers do.

I once enhanced my experience of solidarity with a
small prayer group by making a mental movie. As we
sat, enjoying a silent prayer time together, I pictured
each of us as a photoelectric cell that responds to
sunlight by generating electric power. The Son of God
became the Sun of God in my mind, beaming upon
each of us in that group. In praying, each of us was
investing power into the whole body of which we were
parts.

Electric companies place generating stations at
different strategic points in an interlocking network of
power lines. If there is a breakdown in any part of that
grid, power can shift from a different section of the
country to make up the lack. This is a parable of the
body of Christ. We can be generators when we are
praying for others or speaking words of encouragement
to them. We are putting energy into that network to
which we belong. At other times, when we may be
hurting, we can draw encouragement from the group,
just as a consumer draws electric power from the grid
when he turns on the lights at home.

By deliberately creating mental movies of myself
giving electrical power into the grid, and drawing
some out, I increase my sense of connectedness to the
body of Christ. I am neither a reject, nor a superior,
but an active participant among equals.

Sometimes creating these pictures in our minds
can help us to improve our relationships. A devout
Christian young man lamented that he just couldn't
let go of bitterness he felt about certain mental
wounds he had suffered years earlier. He could quote
Scriptures about how he should forgive but he still

didn't *feel* forgiving. He had prayed repeatedly, "Thank you, God, for letting such-and-such happen in my life." Still, he didn't *feel* thankful.

Then he used the idea that one picture is worth a thousand words. He pictured the wrongs done to him as gashes cutting deeply into his body. Then he imagined himself as a giant key, and those gashes took on new meaning. They were notches precisely machined along the edge of the key, to make it uniquely useful. God could use him as a tool to fit locks that no other key could budge.

The locks represented bitterness, fear, and discouragement in the minds of other people. He could understand them. The hurts in his life had shaped him to be useful in other's lives. He wept and laughed as he visualized God's huge hands turning him, the key, in those locks and freeing others from their mental bondage.

Another time I met a sincere Christian woman who knew many passages of Scripture, and often had deep, personal experiences of worship and closeness to God. Yet she repeatedly fell into the old habit of criticizing her family members. When they would start being noisy, or weren't doing what she wanted them to do, she would lash out in a biting, sarcastic, hurtful way toward her husband and her children. Then she would say again and again, "God, please forgive me. I know I shouldn't do that. I try, but I can't help myself. I want to hold my tongue, but I also want to give in to the temptation and blow up just like my mother used to do."

Her breakthrough came in a psychotherapy session in which she visualized that she was a little child again, and that her mother and father were arguing. She saw their mouths and tongues multiplied and falling out on the ground, going two-forty, biting, and chattering. They looked like the wind-up teeth people can buy in novelty stores. She saw millions of these lying around on the ground, and noticed that she as a child had picked one up and stuffed it into her own mouth. This *borrowed* mouth and tongue is what she used any time she criticized her family. It was not hers in the first place. She borrowed it from Mom and Dad.

Next, she visualized Jesus entering the picture, with her now as a grown woman. Jesus was available to take care of that mouth and tongue. As He stood there with His hands open, she took out that old mouth and tongue and put it into His hands. He took it like a lump of clay, squeezed it in His powerful hands, and molded it into something new.

Then she thought of the Scripture where Isaiah says, "Behold I am a man of unclean lips and I come from a people of unclean lips" (Isaiah 6:5). What did Isaiah do in his faith-imagination? He saw a seraphim, an angelic creature, take a hot coal from a burning altar and put the coal on his lips to purify them.

The woman loved that Scripture and applied it to herself. She saw a hot coal disinfect the hole in her face, and then Jesus put in a new mouth and a new tongue. And what was its quality? Instead of criticism, it spoke words of sweetness and praise. She was able to connect this mental movie with specific Scriptures that she knew and loved. The next week she reported to her therapist, "You wouldn't believe how different my husband is this week!"

There are times, though, when all of the imagination in the world will not correct a situation. Fractured relationships can only be fully healed by the asking and granting of forgiveness.

CHAPTER EIGHT

Stepping-Stones to Forgiveness

*I*magine it is a Sunday morning. You have just entered a uniquely honest worship service at The First Church of the Strong-Willed. As their first hymn, the congregation sings lustily, "My hope is built on nothing less than my old hurts and bitterness."

Strong-willed adults often cling to unforgiveness as if it were life itself. They fear they will die if they let go of their bitterness. And in a sense, they are absolutely correct! They *will* die — to the security that keeps them shrouded in a hard, unyielding shell. People often say in counseling that they think they have committed the unpardonable sin. Upon questioning, though, they usually reveal an unwillingness to forgive God or someone else. While it will not ultimately condemn them to eternity separated from God, an unwillingness to participate in the process of forgiveness will block the forgiveness they could receive so freely from Him now.

When Jesus gave the Lord's Prayer, He made a little commentary afterward. He could have commented on any number of those exquisite statements in His concise, model conversation with God. But the one He picked out was the part about forgiving debts. Right after He said "Amen," He said that if we don't forgive our debtors, our heavenly Father won't forgive us.

I used to have trouble with that apparent tit-for-tat approach on God's part. He seemed kind of small, like a kid on a playground saying, "You make the first move, and then I will do my part." That did not fit the great God who split the Red Sea. Then I realized it is not that God refuses or holds back from forgiving me, but literally, in the nature of things, He cannot forgive me until I have forgiven someone else. God opens His arms wide to embrace me, and for me to embrace Him in a hug of reconciliation and forgiveness.

There is no way I can join in that hug as long as I am holding in my arms a list of grievances, a stack of IOU's, a ledger of accounts receivable from my debtors. I have a choice to make. I can hang on and cherish those grudges, those hurts, those resentments from the past, or I can drop them and receive the embrace from God. He waits. He says, "As long as you are holding on to those, there is no way you and I can get together. It is up to you. I am willing." But God cannot force His forgiveness on someone who does not choose forgiveness.

When we refuse to forgive, the strong-willed child within us clings to childish attitudes and resentments. Yet the apostle Paul tells us, "When I was a child I talked like a child, I thought like a child, I reasoned like a child; now that I have become a man, I am done with childish ways and have put them aside" (1 Corinthians 13:11, NASB).

Many people never leave childish ways behind them because they vengefully refuse to do their mothers and fathers the honor of forgiving them. Staying stuck in childhood by resenting Mom and Dad is something Satan has a heyday with. He steers us away from saying, "Well, Mom and Dad did the best they could. They gave me what they knew how to give me, and I love them. I accept them the way they were. In fact, I specifically appreciate the way they taught me."

For persons feeling a lot of bitterness, those words

stick right below the Adam's apple. That is because Satan is propagandizing, saying, "Look out. If you dare appreciate your parents, you will be under their heel. They'll crush you. You'll be under their power."

That is not true. The way we stay under their power is by believing the delusion that if we rebel and resent them hard enough and long enough, we can declare our own power. But when we continue to fight skirmishes in a war that is finished, we are not free to live life.

The way of life is to accept our parents for who they were and what they did for us, and to forgive them for who they weren't and what they did not do for us. Modern medicine and psychology are discovering that resentment affects the tissues of our bodies, and shortens our lives. When we honor our father and mother, we let go of resentment. We forgive them and we are free; the tissues of our bodies are free from the continual drip of acid inside of us.

Yet forgiveness is often a process, and it's seldom easy. Psychotherapists make their living helping people to struggle through the process, which is a lot like mourning. Both forgiveness and grief involve letting go of something old in order to appropriate something new. Like any difficult task, both can be handled more easily if taken one step at a time.

The first step in both processes is to *acknowledge the situation*. When it comes to grieving, acknowledging the loss means there was something really wanted that is gone. Roger always wanted a dad who would sit down with him and teach him how to use tools. In his fantasy Dad would say, "Son, here is how you do this. Here is how you do that. Now you try it. No, no, not quite like that. That was close. Do it more like this. That's it! You're doing it!" That was Roger's dream. That dream did not come true. He acknowledges that it did not, and that his heart still yearns for it.

In order for me to move from grief to forgiveness, I must acknowledge that the offender broke God's law, and hurt me in the process. It's an important test for me. If the other person merely failed to satisfy my preferences, but did not violate God's laws, I have no case. When the offender really did wrong in God's eyes, I must agree with God, and not whitewash it.

To increase the therapeutic impact of acknowledging the wrong done to me, I can add a mental movie to my thoughts. I see a courtroom in heaven. The wrong done against me has just been described. The evidence is all in. God, Moses and a million angels raise their hands in a vote of "Guilty!" against my offender. I see myself raising my hand along with them all, agreeing with God's verdict in the matter. I am allying with God, rather than pursuing a private vendetta of my own.

The second step is to *admit my own tender feelings*, to go beyond the resentment, beyond the anger. Those are surface feelings that cover deeper feelings of sadness or love. Perhaps a woman remembers, "When Dad was mean to me, my heart broke. How sad that was. I so much wanted his love and his understanding, and he didn't show it to me that time that he hit me."

Perhaps a man admits how much he admired Dad, his manliness, his tool chest, his ability with his hands. He could fix anything. What a marvelous man he was, and how much his son really loved and admired him. Love is always beneath bitterness; otherwise there wouldn't be so much energy in our resentment. We can resent only those things that we once treasured.

In step two, we admit that our hurt was not so much a sting as it was a deep sense of loss. In the heavenly courtroom of our mental movie, in front of the same heavenly jury, I can imagine myself reaching into my wallet and pulling forth an old photograph of the loved one who hurt me long ago. I can see myself revealing to those witnesses that I secretly cherished that memento all these years.

The third step in dealing with my grief and forgiving the one who grieved me is to *absorb the loss.* One version of the Lord's Prayer says, "Forgive us our debts as we forgive our debtors." It is probably wired into us that there is a law of indebtedness: when someone has wronged me, that person is in my debt, and a record needs to be set straight. When I am vengeful I am insisting on settling that account. I am getting even. But when I forgive and absorb the loss, I say, "All right, Dad did wrong me, but I no longer require repayment from him. I'm going to absorb that loss. Yes, I was hurt, but I will let the buck stop here."

That's what Jesus did at the cross. God absorbed the loss of our sin, our wrongs against Him, our breaches of relationship with Him. By His own choice, He loves us and does not want to be cut off from us. He says, "Rather than just whip them and get back at them I will absorb the loss. It is costly to Me to have them break off their relationships with Me, but I willingly pay that price Myself." That is the meaning of Christ's death. When we were bankrupt, Jesus paid the price. He said, "I will absorb the loss in My own body and not require it of them."

So I say of Dad when I absorb the loss, "All right, I don't require any restitution from him. I wipe the slate clean. His balance is now set to zero. He owes me nothing for what he has done." I choose never again to use my loss as a kind of I.O.U. No bargaining, like, "Because you didn't give me such-and-such dream, at least you owe me a loan to help me buy this car that I need. After all the wrong you did to me, now you *have* to do something good for me." No. His debt to me is cancelled. He owed me $10,000, and I say to him, "As of today you no longer owe me a single dollar. I am going to bear that cost." I admit that I will never have what I wanted, and I accept that. I am emptyhanded. I have no claim, no leverage with which to recover damages.

Then, as a visual aid to my decision to absorb the loss, I can imagine Jesus walking toward me out of that crowd of courtroom witnesses. He comes as the expert on absorbing losses. He is now going to entrust me, as His faithful disciple, with some similar work to do.

He hands me a sponge. Then He points to a puddle of spilled milk that symbolizes the wrong done against me. I step forward, kneel, and soak that sponge thoroughly with the spilled milk. I walk over to a convenient porthole that leads to the Lake of Fire. I wring the sponge dry into that porthole, knowing that the milk of malice is incinerated forever. Three times I sponge and wring. The third time, the puddle is totally dry; not a trace remains. As an agent of Christ, I have shown the whole assembly that my offender owes me nothing and has no mess to clean up.

The fourth step to forgiveness is to *abandon the use of memory as a weapon*. People often say, "I can forgive, but I just can't forget." Of course, we cannot forget. God has made us so that anything that has ever happened to us is indelibly recorded in biochemical tissue in our brains. We cannot forget. Memory is a gift from God. Therefore, the only choice we have is what use we will make of our memory — will we harm or heal? Before forgiving we use our memory as a weapon, or as a means of leverage against our offender. In forgiving, I have the memory of a wrong done to me. To abandon the use of it as a weapon, I decide I will never again, even in the heat of an argument, mention the wrong that Dad did to me, in such a way as to punish him, or twist his arm, or make him look bad. I am just removing that from my arsenal as if it had never happened.

It helps to imagine a particular memory I cannot forget, as if it were an arrow in the quiver of my mind. I lift it out, take it in my two hands, break it, and drop it into the nearby Lake of Fire that consumes it forever.

One way to help make forgiveness a permanent transaction is by making myself *accountable* to the person I am forgiving. I can bind myself to my offender, for example, by saying, "I promise to never again mention this matter in such a way as to hurt you. If it ever seems to you that I am bringing it up to use it against you, will you please tell me so, and remind me of this promise?"

The final step of forgiveness, is *appreciation*. Since we cannot forget what has happened to us, our only choice is how we will use our memories. Having ruled out using them as weapons, we leave open to ourselves their use as building blocks only. We focus now on redeeming the valuable aspects of the painful experiences. Earlier, we turned *from de*struction. Now we turn *to con*struction.

Appreciation is the antidote for the poison of bitterness. By appreciating I move out of the old, letting go of all the bitterness, and move into the new, laying hold of the relationship that God had wanted me to have with Him from the start. This is where I finally join with what God has been doing. He knew what I was going through, and He loved me. He was able to spare me from the hardship that I underwent. But He didn't. He allowed me to experience the mom who hit me, or the dad who didn't teach me how to use tools, or the older brother who did not encourage my manhood. God allowed all that for a purpose: to groom me into something.

Now I stop and think what there might be about that difficult experience that I can genuinely appreciate. I search to find something I will give thanks for even before I *feel* thankful. Giving thanks is a step of faith and obedience. That is something I can do even when I don't want to. We are not hypocritical when we give thinks even though we don't *feel* thankful. God commands us to give thanks. Hypocrisy means that we claim to follow a certain authority, then don't. Our feelings are not to be our guide and god; Jehovah is our God, and He says, "In everything give thanks" (1 Thessalonians 5:18 KJV).

So, I go ahead and *try* to be appreciative, and what do I hear in my head? "Well, I am pretty sure this one doesn't qualify. This wound was worse than any other that has ever happened to anybody. I am sure there is nothing anybody could appreciate about the horrible hardship and unique abuse that I alone have suffered."

But then I deliberately reflect, "OK, God, thank You for that situation, for that particular episode I am remembering when Mom hit me. That really hurt. But thank You for what You were teaching me in that situation. In fact, now that I think of it, I was being kind of irresponsible around then. Thank You that Mom cared enough to do something to let me know how I was acting, that my behavior was unacceptable.

And even the times when she was just outright wrong and unfair to me, and my punishment was unjust, thank You for giving me a little bit of an experience that would help me understand what Your Son went through in being tried and killed for a crime that He did not commit. Thank You for giving me that privilege long ago as a kid, and giving me this memory that is still with me to help me understand Your heart and Your program a little better. You really did something for me! I worship You in a whole new way. I feel larger and more insightful than I ever did before. I appreciate that painful thing that happened to me long ago."

When applying appreciation to my grief, I appreciate that, while I mourn the loss, it *was* a loss. I lost a dream. But I remember little snatches of it that I did have. Then I muse, "God, I thank You for the times that Dad showed me how to use a screwdriver. I sure wish he also would have shown me how to use the electric drill, the hammer, and those 14 different kinds of saws that he had. Anyway, I do remember the time he taught me how to use a screwdriver, and taught me the difference between a Phillips head and a regular head. I always think of that every time I use a Phillips screwdriver." It may sound funny to say something that specific and that tiny, but when we do, that's when we weep. It is the specific, little things that touch us.

These steps to forgiveness are no cure-all. You may try them and somewhere along the line, you may hit a roadblock. You might go ahead and mechanically say the words, but something inside of you says, "No, I am not going to admit that I really love Dad. I just can't bring myself to say that."

When you come to a block like that, welcome it as a great opportunity to learn a little bit more about yourself. Deliberately exaggerate that block, that resistance, that reluctance. Go even further with it. Feed it. Say things like, "I *will* not. Never in a thousand years. I don't care how God bakes me in hell, or whatever He does to me. I'll never, never, never admit that I love my father, because if I did that it would be as if I were really reaching out and touching Dad, and that I vow in my deepest soul to strictly refuse forevermore. World without end. Amen."

What may come into focus is a picture of what you

hunger for, what you wanted that you have not yet let yourself know. If you exaggerate your oyster of resentment, you can discover the pearl it hides. Let your pain and resentment be symptoms of the love and desire you once felt. Admit it to yourself first, then to God, and then to the person. If your parents have died, you can still do this in a psychodrama. Put an empty chair in front of you and imagine your father there, and tell him you love him. Talk it back and forth. It helps if you do that with someone else, especially with a trained person who can foster you to say it and finish your grieving.

Years ago, there was a country song called, "I'm My Own Grandpa." What I do to break the chain of iniquity in the curse of the generations is essentially to become my own grandfather. As long as I nurse resentment and bitterness, I am in a child-to-child sibling rivalry with the immature part of my parents.

But as soon as I express heartfelt appreciation to my father, for example, I am feeding that starving part of him that his parents did not feed. So I break myself out of the chain by going back a link and feeding the link ahead of me. I am honoring my father and my mother by not insisting that they give to me, but by giving to them the manna of acceptance that everybody is hungry for. What I wanted *from* them I give *to* them. Then I am free.

Say your eulogy to your loved ones while they are still available. If your parents are still living, go to them and tell them the precious memories you have. This is an important way of forgiving them, of saying goodbye to them now, so that, at the time of their funeral, you won't say, "If only I would have told them so-and-so." Do it now.

I did this some years ago with my mom and dad. I went to them, saw them together, and told them all the precious specific memories that I have about them. A particularly special one I told them was this: "Dad, I remember one time when I must have been about three or four years old. It was a Sunday, because you were sitting there reading the big newspaper you had in your lap. I was across the room from you, pushing the vacuum cleaner back and forth, with the cord all wound up, not plugged in. I was pretending to vacuum, playing house, helping Mom.

"I remember as clear as a bell, Dad, that you laid your paper down on your lap, and looked at me with strength and love in your face, and said, 'Den, why don't you plug the cord in and really vacuum?' I want you to know how proud I was, that my dad thought I was grown up enough to help Mom really vacuum."

When I told him that, his eyes filled. He said he did not remember the time, but he was glad that I told him.

Tell them while they are still alive. It will be a great pleasure to them, but it will be far more important for you. It is more blessed to give than to receive.

In addition to forgiving others, we all face a key decision: whether or not we will forgive God. We could file a damage suit against Him in the Universal Court of Appeals. There we can press for vindication, for a verdict against God, finding Him guilty of gross negligence in the line of duty, since He so blatantly blundered in inflicting our particular parents upon us.

Our alternative is to accept His plan for our lives. To do this we can picture ourselves with Him in heaven before our birth, consenting to be delivered as vulnerable infants into the care of such faulty parents as Mom and Dad were.

We shed shackles when we actually say some words like these: "God, I agree to be a small girl, in the home of a hard father who tells me he would rather have had a son, and I am willing to be overprotected by an anxious mother who deprives me of the chance to learn grown-up skills at an early age. In short, I consent to have You entrust my well-being to amateurs.

"God of Abraham, Isaac, Jacob, Mom and Dad, and me, what a fantastic program You have under way. What liberty You give me even to thumb my nose at You, to say 'no' to Your outreaching arms. I really crack when I run that kind of risk with people, and they say 'no' to me. But what a security it is to know that You are not fragile; that You don't take insult, but that You find new, creative ways to come around and caress me, and invite me to You.

"Thank You for Your creativity in the cross, where Your Son, Jesus, in Whose name I address You, said, 'Father, forgive them. They just don't realize what they are doing."

CHAPTER NINE

Contentment Through Repentance

*S*trong-Willed Adult: Please forgive me.
    God: For what wrong?
Strong-Willed Adult: Oh, I lost my temper at the kids.
    God: So what?
Strong-Willed Adult: What do you mean?
    God: What was wrong about losing your temper at the kids?
Strong-Willed Adult: Well, You don't want me to, do You?
    God: You're not answering the question I asked you.
Strong-Willed Adult: What did You ask me?
    God: What was wrong about losing your temper at the kids?
Strong-Willed Adult: You're telling me now that it wasn't wrong?
    God: I didn't say that. I am asking you what you think was wrong about losing your temper at the kids.
Strong-Willed Adult: Look, I'm sorry! All right? What more does a guy hafta do, bleed or something?
    God: No, that's already been taken care of.
Strong-Willed Adult: Well, what am I supposed to do?
    God: To accomplish what?
Strong-Willed Adult: To be forgiven for blowing up at the kids.

God: Tell me what you think was wrong about blowing up at the kids.

Strong-Willed Adult: All right, it was wrong because I shouldn't do it.

God: Why not?

Strong-Willed Adult: You are really confusing me. Here I am, apologizing for breaking one of Your rules, and You're giving me a hard time over it.

God: Do you know what's really happening between us?

Strong-Willed Adult: No, what?

God: I am asking you a question that is right at the center of your request to me. And you, instead of taking the question seriously and doing the hard work of thinking about it, are accusing Me of mistreating you.

Strong-Willed Adult: I'm sorry.

God: For what wrong?

Strong-Willed Adult: Oh, no, here we go again. Can't You just say, "OK, I forgive you for accusing Me"?

God: Forgiveness is a meeting of two minds, agreeing on the nature of some wrong that was done. So far, you have not made clear to Me what you think was wrong about losing your temper at the kids.

Strong-Willed Adult: Well, *You* think it was wrong, don't You?

God: You tried that one on Me already.

Strong-Willed Adult: What do You mean?

God: You already tried to toss the ball to Me and get Me to bawl you out, instead of you answering the question of what was wrong about blowing your top at the kids.

Strong-Willed Adult: OK, I give up. What do You want from me?

God: This conversation started with you wanting something from Me, remember? I am still ready to hear your request. I'm just not yet clear on what you consider to be the basis for your request, or why you even think one is in order. To be specific, what was there about losing your temper at the kids that would call for Me to forgive you?

Strong-Willed Adult: You mean You're not mad at me?

God: You just did it again.

Strong-Willed Adult: Did what?

God: Changed the subject instead of answering the question.

Strong-Willed Adult: Boy, You are really being rough on me, just trying to make me bow and scrape and beat my breast in contrition, eat crow and humble pie. All right, if that's what You want, I'll do it — sackcloth and ashes, the whole bit!

God: Whoops! Mistaken identity.

Strong-Willed Adult: Huh?

God: You are portraying Me as the kind of villain you considered your mother and father to be when you felt guilty around them.

Strong-Willed Adult: I am?

God: Isn't that what you always resented about them? Didn't it seem to you that they were mostly interested in knowing you suffered for the things you did that they didn't like? Didn't they work harder to prove they were in the right than to help you learn principles from your mistakes, things that would help you to think your way through new situations you would face in the future?

Strong-Willed Adult: Yeah, now that You mention it, I always did hate that about them.

God: And now you approach Me in the posture of a guilty wrongdoer, predicting that I will react in the same way Mom and Dad did.

Strong-Willed Adult: Well, You *are* reacting just like them.

God: Only in your eyes. When you ask Me to forgive you, and I ask you what you think was wrong about what you did, you think I am kind of roasting you like your parents used to. Kind of making you stew in your humiliation, prolonging your agony so as to feel Myself to be some kind of a victor over you. Right?

Strong-Willed Adult: Yes, that's exactly what I think You are doing.

God: Fine, we agree on what *you* think I am doing. Now I will tell you what *I* think I am doing. I, unlike your imperfect biological parents whom I also love, am respecting your intellect, your opinions and views. I am talking with you in such a way as to bring forth from you the finest qualities that I put in you when I designed you. I am telling you I am interested in the results of your *thinking*. I truly am looking forward to comparing our views and showing you My ways, so you can consider them and see if you want to adopt them as *your* ways, by your own free choice.

Strong-Willed Adult: Hmm, what You're saying sounds good, but...

God: But you're not sure you can trust Me yet, not to lose My temper at you?

Strong-Willed Adult: Yes, that's right.

God: Does that give you any ideas about what might be wrong about your losing your temper at your kids?

Ever hear an empty "I'm sorry"? What the person means is, "Please let me off the hook even though I reserve the right to continue abusing you in the future." That person wants relief from the consequences of wronging you, without changing the conditions that resulted in your hurt.

God hears these hollow pleas all the time. Note His policy on them: "If we [freely] admit that we have sinned and confess our sins, He is faithful and just [true to His own nature and promises] and will forgive our sins (dismiss our lawlessness) and continuously cleanse us from all unrighteousness — everything not in conformity to His will in purpose, thought and action" (1 John 1:9, Amplified).

God forgives us when we *confess*, not when we ask. Hear that again: the precondition for our forgiveness is not that we ask to be forgiven, but that we confess our sins. The effective words are not, "I am sorry," but, "I was wrong." In fact, we even commit sin when we pray to be forgiven. To beg God, "Please forgive me," is to imply that we have to give Him the idea or He won't think of it. Or perhaps it reveals that we think He has to be coaxed in order to relent and let us off the hot seat.

But the familiar Scripture above says it is God's nature to forgive. He is like a loaded gun just waiting to go off with an explosion of joy. The trigger is our confession of wrongdoing. As soon as we admit our sin, He forgives us. If we add in there, "Please forgive me," we are interrupting Him. It's like pulling the trigger on a shotgun, feeling the recoil against your shoulder, then saying, "I sure hope this thing goes off."

Hand-in-glove with confessing goes the necessity of repenting, of turning around and going the other way. John the Baptist was most insightful concerning the necessity and potency of rock-bottom repentance in a person's life (Luke 3:3-14). To him it constituted (a) clearsighted awareness of the ghastly awfulness of my wrongdoing, in the light of God's holy nature; (b) a feeling of abhorrence for my past wrongs; (c) utterly renouncing my past ways, in favor of (d) hearty commitment to specific, regular conduct that is righteous before God, and generous, fair, and gentle toward my fellow people. My new life is also to be marked by my repeated choice to be content with what I have in the way of earthly provisions, and to express appreciation and good will instead of griping.

Like forgiveness, repentance can best be explained as a step-by-step process. The first step is to *acknowledge* the specific thing I did that was wrong. Not just, "I blew my top at the kids," but, "God, I yelled at Susie and called her stupid. I pushed Jimmy and said I wanted him out of my sight. Then when my wife came in to calm me down, I swore at her and blamed her for the kids' misbehavior." The key to this step is viewing my own actions through the eyes of those I affected.

In this example from everyday family life, it would be appropriate for me to go to the persons I have offended and confess to them. But how might I apply this first step to the larger issue of struggling against God's authority? In that case, I would acknowledge, "God, I have conducted myself as if You were weak, stupid and mean, instead of powerful, wise and good. I have resented human authorities over me and have sought to defeat them when I did not like the way they were leading. I have continued to use in adult life the maneuvers I learned as a strong-willed child refusing to respect any authority higher than my own."

The second step is to *assess the impact* of my actions and attitudes on others. Industrial corporations must file with the U.S. government an environmental impact assessment for any major project they undertake, like building an electrical power plant. We are all part of a spiritual ecology. What we do and say cannot help but have an impact on our fellow humans *and* our Creator.

To properly assess that impact, I must relive it all in their shoes. "I realize that I broke my mother's heart when I told her I did not care what she thought, but that I was going to do what *I* wanted."

"The wrong thing about my constant complaining around my wife is that I starve her of the encouragement that would lighten her load and brighten her enthusiasm for her God-ordained role as wife and mother."

"My offense to God in my stubbornness has been that I have rebuffed the love that He stood ready to lavish upon me. I have done nothing less than fight against the very machinery by which the universe operates. I have cast my vote with those who murdered Jesus, when they said, 'We will not have this Man to rule over us.'"

The third step in repentance is to *about face*. It is the crux of repentance. In steps one and two, I confessed explicitly the direction I have been going and what was ungodly about it. Now I pivot 180 degrees and point in the opposite direction. Here is where I tell what I would do differently if I had it to do over again.

Genuine guilt reflects such a horror for what I have done to others that I would in no way repeat my offense if given the chance to do so again. What would I do instead?

"God, if I could go back to my teen-age years with Mom, instead of breaking off from her for being domineering, I would tell her I intend to obey her as the mother God put in authority over me. And I would tell her she could make it easier for me to obey her joyfully if she would take time to explain to me calmly the reasons behind the rules she was laying down for me."

The fourth step is to *consider if there is anything else*. We don't want premature sutures over wounds that are not yet disinfected. We make sure to get all the poison out. One of the best ways to check is to relive our old hurtful memories, and see if we still feel some bites of bitterness. Then we can confess and repent our own prideful reactions to those difficulties that God allowed into our lives long ago. We can use our false guilts here. They are like stones in a forest.

Turn over a stone of guilt and you find on the secret
side of it creepy crawly grubs of resentment.

The fifth step in repentance is to *make ourselves
accountable* to God. In doing so we activate an alarm
system to alert ourselves to any recurrence of the
wrongs we have repented. We do this best by putting
to new use some existing raw materials close at hand.
Our *feelings* of guilt or resentment now become our
servants instead of our masters.

We now respect these feelings as warning signals
God has wired into us, like the red lights on the
dashboard of a car. When one goes on we immediately
speak to our new Father and say, "Oh, oh. Something's
going on here that threatens to interfere with our close
walk together. What am I doing to activate the
signals?" God respects our intellect, and He jumps at
the chance to sharpen our understanding and lead us
ever deeper into those thoughts of His which up till
now could not have become our thoughts. We can
thank Him for creating such sensitive consciences.

Once we have taken the necessary steps to confess
and repent, all we must do is receive the forgiveness
God so freely gives. But for the strong-willed person,
that doesn't always come easy.

In her classic book, *The Christian's Secret of A
Happy Life*, Hannah Whitall Smith quotes a strong-
willed child who insisted that God does not forgive us
immediately upon our confessing, but requires
considerable suffering from us first. The child
maintained, "I believe that *is* the way He does...no
matter what the Bible says."

Like many strong-willed adults, that little girl
would rather suffer by her timetable than be forgiven
by God's. Her self put-down was really an attempt to
regulate God, since she preferred her own conclusions
over God's authoritative promises.

The path to contentment and true self-love lies in

accepting God's contradiction of our ideas, and welcoming His discipline and acknowledging His terms for relating to Him. His are much kinder than ours. But this is not to say that we cannot seek to understand *why* God chooses to order our lives the way He does. He *invites* our honest protests.

Consider Job, who expressed his suffering honestly and openly: "If I called, and He answered me, yet would I not believe that He listened to my voice" (Job 9:16, Amplified). What a strong-willed flavor that statement has! Is Job neurotic? His complaints resemble the neurotic's reproaches against fate, life, and God. But notice a different character to his words as he continues in his anguish: "I am weary of my life, and loathe it! I will give free expression to my complaint; I will speak in the bitterness of my soul. I will say to God, 'Do not condemn me — do not make me guilty! Show me why You contend with me'" (Job 10:1, 2, Amplified).

Perhaps Job's words are a model of honest wrestling with God by a man who is afflicted, who is trying to make sense of his affliction, and who is calling boldly for an encounter with the living God. From the rest of Job's monologues we recognize his reverence for God. He does not deny God's right to run the universe, as does the neurotic who strives for the throne. Job simply states how rough it is for him to undergo the treatment that God has every right to allow. Job asks for a response from God, not an excuse or apology. Job wants more to understand than to overrule God's ways.

Another sufferer, a psalmist, occasionally blurts out his candid displeasure toward God. The result is that he soon clears his vision and remembers that God *is* God. Note Psalm 10, verse 1: "Why do You stand afar off, O Lord?" Then the psalmist's perspective in verse 16: "The Lord is King for ever and ever." Again

Psalm 13:1 complains, "How long will You forget me, O Lord? For ever? How long will You hid Your face from me?" Then in verse 6, the gloom dissolves in gratitude; "I will sing to the Lord, because He has dealt bountifully with me."

This kind of anger in relating to God is far different from our wounded-pride anger in which we want to break off relations with God. He has wired into us a way to gain perspective and relief. If we will genuinely wrestle with Him, candidly gripe to His face about how He is treating us, the inevitable result is a meeting of the minds. We come to our senses and recognize how vast and how approachable He is. As our vision of His greatness enlarges, the scope of our upset grows less.

CHAPTER TEN

Developing Spiritual Muscle

*I*magine what would happen to a marathon runner who trained for a big race merely by eating the right foods. The runner would be emphasizing only part of a truth: muscle tissue does need input of proper nutrition. The whole truth is that healthy muscles require nourishment, rest and exercise.

Spiritually, we are like muscle. We do need nourishment from our relationship with God. We need recognition from others. We also need rest in the form of occasional solitude. But most of all, we need exercise to keep us strong and healthy.

In this chapter we are going to explore three kinds of spiritual exercise that will help us in our walk of faith and will keep us from falling into the flabbiness of our old, strong-willed natures. The first exercise is *practicing the art of contributing to others.*

My wife, Ruth, and I have moved six times during our married life. Each time, Ruth has readily made new friends by putting on coffees for them. As a newcomer, she puts on coffees for the people who already live there! She often listens to other women who have moved several times and feel bruised at having to leave their friends. They move into a new neighborhood and wait for people to approach them.

Ruth is always amazed when she hears these women complain that their neighborhoods are un-friendly. "How can any neighborhood be unfriendly if *you* are in it?" She asks. "How can you allow a neighborhood to stay unfriendly since you have it in your power to extend your friendship? And if at least one person, you, is extending friendship, can the neighborhood be called 'unfriendly' anymore?"

It *is* more blessed to give than to receive, to be a host than a guest. It is more rewarding, more personally satisfying, more fulfilling, more actively zesty to give than it is to receive or to hold on to what we already have.

Recipes routinely require a pinch of salt because it brings out the unique flavor of each of the other ingredients. What does a pinch of *you* do for a recipe of people of which you are a part? Jesus said you are the salt of the earth (Matthew 5:13). Note, not "you *should* be," not "try to be," but, "you *are* the salt of the earth." Salt is an intrusive ingredient in a recipe and its presence improves the whole meal.

We do not just leak through life. We go about actively putting forward, flinging forth, ejecting, radiating a particular kind of influence, expression, or assertion. It can be nourishing or toxic, a constructive contribution or a destructive diminution toward those around us.

It was this constructive contribution that Jesus offered wherever He went. Yet dubious, hostile, and even religious critics quizzed Him on His every move. One time they asked why He was consorting with an ill-reputed crowd (Luke 5:30). They wondered what He *got* out of associating with sinners. Jesus answered in terms of what He *gave*. His motivation for mingling was to contribute to their well-being, not to take selfish advantage of their admiration to boost His own superiority.

The robes people wore in Jesus' time were more than just clothing. The bosom of a robe formed a pouch often used as a bag. With it, the wearer could deliver and receive goods in bulk, such as grain. It was the convenient Mediterranean measuring cup. Jesus used it as an object lesson about generosity: "For with the measure you deal out — that is, with the measure you use when you confer benefits on others — it will be measured back to you" (Luke 6:38, Amplified).

The reservoir is the same; it has a two-way use. Only in the outgoing direction is it stretchable. The extent to which we stretch our pouch of generosity to others establishes the maximum abundance we are later able to receive. Jesus applied this principle particularly to generous forgiving. There He said, "Acquit and forgive and release (give up resentment, let it drop), and you will be acquitted and forgiven and released" (Luke 6:37, Amplified).

See it in your mind's eye. You are wearing a robe, size: extra-large. You are using it as a pouch at chest level, to hold several pounds of moldy, smelly grain. At a beckoning from Jesus, you let it drop. The robe falls flat against your skin. The rotten grain falls to the ground. What a relief! Your arms are now free to embrace that handsome, smiling Savior! Then you fluff your robe into a large pouch, to take in His lavish outpouring of the sweetest-tasting bread you've ever known. It is the Bread of Life.

Jesus repeatedly prescribed outgoing generosity as the heart of happy living. In Luke 10, he plugged it from three different angles. First, He cited as the essence of the grand Hebrew tradition, descended from Moses, that we are to love God and our neighbors heartily (Luke 10:27).

Then He told the Good Samaritan story. Its moral is that we are to align ourselves with God's merciful heart by investing ourselves in alleviating the conditions of people upon whom misfortunes have fallen through no lapse or laziness of their own. Finally (Luke 10:38-42), the Master urged His friend, Martha, to involve herself more in here-and-now relationships with eternal matters than with material preparations. Like a wise and gentle daddy, He disarmed her self-imposed martyrdom. He lightheartedly rebuked Martha and praised her sister.

This was loving admonition in action. Martha was using the classic strong-willed gambit of harried busyness, to extort approval from others, and to coerce her sister to come under her command. She sought superiority through suffering; Jesus offered her partnership through participation.

There can be a difference between giving and contributing. Giving often implies that the other person is obligated to receive. That is not the kind of giving that is more blessed than receiving. It is actually another form of receiving. It is counterfeit generosity. It has a string attached. It is a payment in a deal: "Because I have been so kind to you, you are now duty-bound to show me your gratitude. You owe me appreciation. You *must* confess that I have done a wonderful deed." Contributing means freely offering what I have, no strings or expectations attached. I leave it as if deposited in God's hands, for Him to do with as He sees fit. He is the God of the harvest, free to multiply a hundredfold, or to parch the seedlings in a rainless summer.

Jesus knew what was the unthinkable catastrophe in the life of the rich young ruler who dabbled in spiritual interests. He prescribed for that fellow (not necessarily for everyone else), "Go and sell what you have, and give to the poor, and you will have riches in heaven; Then come, be My disciple" (Matthew 19:21, Amplified). We can see that young man's face blanch, his jaw drop, and his shoulders droop. "What? Face life without my financial security blanket? Suffer the shocks of life without a credit card cushion? I couldn't stand it."

Note that Jesus did not just lay this heavy confrontation on this wealthy man uninvited. The man had asked what he could do to belong to the exquisite assembly of likeminded people who thrill to the presence of God through all eternity. The Savior leaked a secret: what heaven's inhabitants have in common is an investing mentality. They take initiative to benefit their fellow humans.

Contributing to others presupposes a second spiritual exercise: practicing *self-denial.*

Imagine a hungry farmer in the spring of the year, looking at the grain he has, and thinking how good it would feel to eat it. But he says, "No, we are going to skimp and go hungry for a while. I am going to take that seed and give it away to the ground." That grain would be *so* handy to make into bread and eat right now, to satisfy a temporary hunger.

Instead, the farmer plants it in the ground, not guaranteed what will become of it. It has died as far as he is concerned. He is cooperating with God, doing his part in trusting. The walk of faith involves giving away that which we tend to cling to, as our part in working with God's promise to multiply it.

Jesus had a rather pithy way of inviting followers. He did not make it easy. He made it possible for everyone, yet evidently did not expect His criteria to meet with a majority response. Note how He clearly made it optional: "If any person wills to come after me, let him deny himself — that is, disown himself, forget, lose sight of himself and his own interests, refuse and give up himself — and take up his cross daily, and follow Me [that is, cleave steadfastly to Me, conform wholly to my example, in living and if need be in dying also]. For whoever would preserve his life and save it, will lose and destroy it; but whoever loses his life for My sake, he will preserve and save it [from the penalty of eternal death]" (Luke 9:23, 24, Amplified).

Anyone who chooses to go the way of Jesus finds that His way goes precisely against the human inclination to seek superiority as protection against bruises to self-esteem. His way is to deny one's own status. More than that, His way is to refuse even the effort to feed and protect one's prestige. Instead, the disciple walks daily into the face of humiliation if that be necessary to contribute to the kingdom of God.

"...take up his cross daily..." Think what that means. People get killed on crosses. Worse than that, they suffer intensely for a long time before they die on their crosses. Worse yet, before the spikes enter their flesh, they suffer the searing scorn of onlookers who watch them drag their own instrument of torture and death to the place of execution. They are forced against their wills to perform that most degrading duty. It is public proof that they are defeated, impotent, hated and rejected, worthless non-members being removed from society.

Jesus taught *that* as a manageable way to live. He was more impressed with the worthwhileness of doing kingdom work than He was with the horrors of humiliation. He knew He was about to face the fate we all fear worse than death — rejection. He clearly decided He would not diminish His own continued work for the kingdom, even though He was despised for it by the very authorities with whom He most eagerly wanted to fellowship!

Remember, some of the religious men who called for His crucifixion had probably been in on those exhilarating conversations He had enjoyed for several days in Jerusalem at age 12. So, He denied Himself and took up His cross. He asks *of* us what He willingly did *for* us. Yet it was not easy for Him.

Jesus had less than twenty-four hours to live. He agonized with God in the Garden of Gethsemane (Luke 22:42-44). His intense praying was a mature, manly manifestation of strong revulsion, of which tantrums are a childish counterfeit. Jesus earnestly implored God against the task He perceived God laying before Him.

When Jesus asked God to remove the cup of death, it was a very human request. If there were another way for God to accomplish His purpose, Jesus wanted it. Yet God told Him no, there was no other way. And Jesus accepted the answer, maintained His contact with God, and furthermore affirmed God's plan as the one that would ultimately prevail.

There is a nutritional deficiency in the body of Christ in America today. We lack the trace elements contained in the fruit of the Spirit called "longsuffering." We overindulge on the junk food of shortsuffering. We need to become familiar with *not* getting some of what we urgently want. We need to follow Jesus' example and *practice taking "no" for an answer.*

The mature adult, like Jesus, in the role of subordinate, appeals vigorously to God to modify the orders. Always behind the subordinate's bold, emphatic request is the willingness for God's "no" to be the final and the finest answer. By contrast, strongwilled protests carry the threat that we will break off relations with God if we don't get our way. We thus reveal that the ultimate authority that guides us is our own willful desire.

Note the remarkable calm with which Jesus faced the mockery and abuse that came just hours after His impassioned praying. He obviously was not just resentfully going along with the "no" from God, thinking it a stupid and unfair answer. Instead, He had settled something with God in the garden. He heard more than just, "No, you can't have your way." He recognized that His powerful, wise and good Father was saying, "No, I have something far more splendid in mind for You than just freedom from pain."

One of God's favorite tools for disciplining us is the environment. Bible stories tell of wilderness experiences where men of God grew in wisdom and maturity. When there is no one else around to pamper us, we encounter God's laws of nature as a perfectly consistent parent. At the age of 38, I went on a stress camping expedition in the wilderness, and there watched God tame a large portion of my childish strong will.

As I look back on that profound experience, I see God as my skilled psychotherapist, maneuvering me into an uncomfortable situation that I could get out of only by doing something mature and responsible. I was in a tender trap in which I would be blessed if I complied and blessed if I defied.

My muscles were sore. I was tired and hungry, dirty and thirsty. The bugs droned relentlessly around my head. My repellent did not work against them. I was bored of the monotony of day-after-day backpacking on miles and miles of tedious trails. I hated it. No, that's too mild. I *vowed* my hatred of the program.

I decided I was dumb to have come. I wanted to quit. It was the same futile frustration I remembered as a kid when I was doing poorly at a game and wanted to take my bat and ball and go home. The problem was, in the past I had always been able to get out of hated situations one way or another. I was always able to quit or get an easier assignment. When I had sought special treatment in the past, the answer had always been "yes." Now I was facing "no", and it aroused all my stubborn fury at not being in the driver's seat.

I was deep in the heart of a remote forest, arduous miles from the highways that could get me to the comforts of home. I had only three options for getting out: (1) suicide, (2) making the other four group members carry me, (3) following the program as planned. I had long ago ruled out the question of suicide, so option #1 was not open to me.

If I fell helpless, or sick or otherwise passive, I could probably induce the others to carry my gear and me out of the woods. However, that would mean I would have to trust them. That happened to be one of my strong-willed hang-ups. I preferred to do things *my* way. I did not want to be at the mercy of anyone else's competence. If I chose option #2, I would be under my group's authority. God would use it to break my strong will against trusting others.

My third option was to walk out of the woods on my own power as the Wilderness Seminar required. I knew I was *able* to do that; I just didn't *want* to. It galled me to realize that I was wedged into a corner where the easiest thing for me to do was the thing I hated most to do: obey the rules of an authority I didn't want to follow.

I felt defeated, humiliated, broken. Tantrum anger, my most valued ally, was of no use to me in this pickle. The distance to go was too great for me to make by the temporary adrenalin surge of anger. I was finally in a situation bigger than me.

I had to depend on forces I could not control: my body's metabolism of the food our leaders rationed out, my companions' work in preparing campsites and meals, trail markers and maps made by someone else. My sovereignty was reduced to two menial functions: lifting my weary legs one at a time, and heaving my lungs breath upon breath.

I now look back upon that onerous ordeal as one of the most valuable experiences of my life. I benefitted from it in direct proportion to how savagely I hated it *and did it anyway!* I demanded that God give me an easy way out of the woods. He said "no." I took "no" for my answer, and grew several inches in spiritual stature. I learned to bend to a will higher than my own. I was like a stiff patient coming with atrophied

muscles to a physical therapist. The therapist showed
kindness in making me bend those muscles no matter
how painful. I now have a range of movement I never
knew before.

Another way to exercise our spiritual muscles is
the discipline of refusing food occasionally for a period
of time. At least one godly teacher has advocated
missing breakfast and lunch each Wednesday and
Friday, and praying frequently during those hours for
spiritual revival in our nation.

An obvious caution with fasting is not to substitute credit for calories. We do not discipline ourselves, if, while abstaining from food, we let people
know we are doing it, so that they will admire our
show of righteousness. Then we are merely replacing
one indulgence with another, and allowing ourselves
to remain spiritually flabby.

I have learned something about the value of fasting
along with prayer. When I pray, the only attitude that
is realistic is that God is in charge, and my investment
of time and energy in prayer is for the purpose of His
changing me. This attitude of obedient openness to
Him normally results in my recognition that God is
pushing me to let go of something I've been clinging to
so He can fill my hands with a new treasure. The old
things I cling to usually are my idea of how a task
should be handled, my idea of the best way for me to
use my time...*my* preference, *my* desire, *my* opinion,
my dream.

Recently, my church congregation fasted and
prayed for a week, seeking God's guidance in the
matter of expanding our facilities. To pray wrongly
was easy: "God, please change the minds of these
stubborn people around me, and help them to see the
wisdom and correctness of the solution I have in mind
for this problem." God does not honor that prayer, but
instead leans on me to be openminded, seeking to hear

and consider the proposals of others. To be obedient I
need to let go of my narrowminded insistence that I
am right. This is a death to self; it is giving up my
pride.

To do this, fasting is a great help. Being without
food for a period of time is a parable of letting go. By
fasting I am saying to myself that I am willing to do
without something that is important to me physically.
Thus, I am making it easier to cooperate with God's
initiative, which requires me to let go of my own way.
Fasting is something I do for me, not for God. It is a
specific way in which I prepare to notice and respond
to God's prompting.

The hunger pangs I feel while fasting are to me a
parable of seeking. In my praying, I am hungering and
thirsting after righteousness, after God's way for me to
live. I remind myself that His ways are like food. "Oh,
God, as food satisfies the hunger of my craving body,
so does Your wisdom satisfy the craving of my inner
being."

My recognition of the personal benefit of fasting is
new. In the past, when I read in the Bible of people
praying and fasting, I wrote it off as an ancient
custom, along with sackcloth and ashes. If I pictured
myself fasting at all, it was as a sacrifice I would make
in order to twist God's arm.

We are all prone to abuse godly disciplines, to try
to manipulate God by our sacrifices. Such sacrifices
we intend as dues payments to God so that He comes
into our debt and can be expected to answer our
requests. Sacrifice in this spirit is rebellion; it is
dictating to God how He shall respond to our prayer; it
is competing with God Himself.

By fasting as I pray in earnest, I do myself a favor. I
allow my body to be a continual reminder to me that
my approach to God is on His terms. I remind myself
that I am willing to give up anything that is precious

to me in order to experience the surpassing excellence
of knowing His wisdom and His ways.

CHAPTER ELEVEN

Facing the Bogeyman

*S*uppose you could go back to one nightmare-ridden night of your childhood. You are trembling in your bed. It's nearly pitch dark. Only a trickle of light leaks around the covering over your window. You notice a movement in the darkest part of the room. It is a humpy hulk you have seen before but always managed to send away in the nick of time by a light or a mom summoned to shoo the bogeyman. This time you decide to face him fully, come what may. Sure you shiver, but you decide not to let your fear hold you back. You act even though you are afraid. You say, "Hey you, bogeyman. I'm over here. Come right here where I can see you."

He snarls and lumbers over to you, hoping to scare you under the covers. Instead you get out of bed and stand on the floor to meet him head-on. He shuffles right up to you, growling his foul breath into your face. You stretch your neck forward even further to get a completely detailed view of that fiendish face in the faint light. And wouldn't you know it, he has acne! Bad case of it! No wonder he acts the way he does. He has to scare people off so they won't see him up close. He couldn't bear the embarrassment.

But now you know his long-held secret. He is at your mercy. How are you going to use your power over him? Will you, too, laugh at him as did the others who hurt him long ago? You think of it for a moment. Then your heart melts. You ruffle his hair with one hand, then say, "Well, we've both had a hard night. What do you say we get some shuteye, partner?" Then you crawl back into your bed, and he to his corner, and you both get a long-sought night's rest.

When we deliberately face what we normally avoid, we become different. Facing our fears is another muscle-building technique, one of the most powerful around.

Many of our human fears stem from pride. To the extent that fear is pride, "I can't stand it" translates into "I won't stand for it."

What happens to us in situations we truly cannot stand? We keel over. For example, we cannot stand a lack of oxygen for more than a matter of seconds without passing out. If we have been standing on our feet, we fall down.

But when we say, "I can't stand it," we do not usually mean that we are going to physically faint or die if the current stress continues upon us. What we mean is that we don't like it. We would rather not bear it. It is more than we prefer to endure. And that is where our strong will comes in. In our prideful pretentions to the throne we believe we ought not to have to tolerate what we don't like. We consider ourselves entitled to exemption from exertion.

You can shatter the ice of your own pride by deliberately doing something worthwhile that you fear. If you have been shy, pray in public. If you have resented your parents, or feared their domination, hug them. As you do so, see yourself pulling the fuse out of a bomb labeled "I can't stand it."

One of the things we think we "can't stand" is disapproval. Some people are so fearful of disapproval that they imagine it to be a vicious vampire bat that could drain their life's blood.

Yet Jesus regarded disapproval as more of a mosquito. He recognized that all it can do is buzz around. At worst, it can only give a minor sting — more of an inconvenience than a terror.

Jesus often met with disapproval. One example was the time He arranged dinner at the home of Jericho's Public Enemy Number One, Zacchaeus, the crooked, treasonous tax collector (Luke 19:1-10).

Jesus, the famous and popular wonderworker, faced complaints against doing what He thought was right. Since He was not immune to disapproval, we probably cannot expect to be. Our worth to the human race and to the kingdom of God is not always accurately reflected by the treatment we happen to get at the moment from the crowd at hand.

An act of cowardice by a Roman official allowed the illegal execution of Jesus, the Messiah (Matthew 27:24). Pilate caved in to fear of rejection. Jesus did not. For us to stand courageously for what we believe to be right is not a small thing. Every time we hold firm against intimidation and exercise authority for a just and righteous outcome, we correct for an error that cost Jesus His life. We help to set the human order straight. Not that we undo Pilate's wrong, but we validate the rightness of what he should have done.

How do we get the kind of boldness this requires? Part of the secret lies in exchanging one place of security for another. Peter discovered this one day on Sea of Galilee.

The wind blew more fiercely than it had been blowing a moment before. It splashed the froth of whitecapped waves against Peter's legs as he minced his way toward Jesus. Peter's walk on water (Matthew 14:30) was like what we all experience in maturing. For him there were two places of security, and a solitary journey between them. He was willing to leave the old, familiar security of the smelly fishing boat for the new, thrilling security of companionship with his Master, Jesus. But between the two he was on his own. It was *his* feet that had to take those steps; Jesus would not do it for him. Peter had asked Jesus to beckon him. Jesus had said, "Come," not, "Here, I'll do it for you."

Peter felt the wind and mistakenly took the attitude that circumstances could overwhelm him. "I can't stand it" is the childish way of thinking in all of us that shuts down our bold use of the abilities God has delegated to us. We begin to move toward our attractive companion, Jesus. We also hesitate to leave the familiar, childish, symptomatic ways of coping with life that have been of *some* advantage to us. When we launch out and find ourselves in the wind of adversity, we yield to our neurotic anxiety. We agree with Satan's lie that we "can't stand it."

No question about it: God's way for us, His way of growth, always has with it the temporary, lonely journey through buffeting circumstances. Faith is boldness when we are not secure.

Perhaps you have the good fortune to live with a bogeyman. You may have the opportunity even today to practice an eternally valuable skill. Do something you believe is godly and in the long-term best interest of your relationship, but that you've been holding off doing because you feared your partner's predictable blow-up.

As your partner lashes out, searing you with verbal abuse, notice exactly what it feels like. Instead of fighting it off this time, tune in to exactly what there is about it that is most painful to you. Tolerate the experience, just to see what it is like, and to exercise your muscles for enduring that kind of hardship.

For example, you may be the wife of a man with a short fuse on his temper. Perhaps also he has been more married to his job than to you for many months. You know it would be good for your marriage if he would take you out for a romantic little drive or stroll to a nearby ice cream stand some evening this week. You have not dared to suggest such an idea because you have told yourself you could not possibly endure the overpowering onslaught of his vile rejection of you and your idea.

The neurotic side of us anticipates and arranges failures, to justify not keeping on. Jesus advocated that we seek and keep on seeking; persistence and courage are keys to success (Luke 11:8-10). For example, if you wanted a little ice-cream romance with your husband, you could probably get it if you asked repeatedly in a good-natured manner, and took each of his first fifteen rejections lightly.

"All right, so we can't afford it; let's just window shop." "I know you're busy. That's why it will be an extra special treat to me for you to take me. I really like busy men. It makes them kind of, oh — earthy. That's one of the things I like about you; you're earthy. Come on, take me to the ice cream place."

To speak jovially like that, you would need to take a fresh attitude. In your old frame of mind, as you are reading this book you may be mentally muttering, "It won't work. I tried it and it didn't work."

If we had video tapes of the times you tried to arrange your ice cream dates, we might notice the gloom instead of enthusiasm in the way you approach your husband. We would sense the tentative, halfhearted spirit of your request. Though we would wish to light a firecracker under your husband's affection, we would not be surprised at his lack of response to his wife's feeble invitation.

If our video machine had a crystal ball feature, we might read such thoughts as these in your mind: "It's not fair for me to be the one who does the changing. People ought to make my husband be cheerful to *me*. For me to put my unprotected heart out and honestly ask for what I want and then be turned down is a cruel wound far too severe for me to survive."

Risk it! Deliberately bring that avalanche upon

yourself just to notice that you *do* survive it. Observe
microscopically just how your husband does his
number. Guess at what kind of disasters he feels he
must protect himself against by his bullying. Think of
yourself this time as a vulcanologist who has a first-
hand opportunity to study an erupting volcano from
inside the crater, while wearing an asbestos suit.

Sometimes the bogeyman in our lives is *not* a loved
one. Perhaps he belongs to another group Jesus pin-
pointed for you to invest in — your enemies.

This assignment was not for everyone. Jesus offered it in private conversation reserved for His most
devoted followers. These were the ones who accepted
when He said, *"If* any person will follow me..." To
this "in" group He offered a four-way formula to un-
bogey the bogeyman (Matthew 5:44, Luke 6:27, 28).

Picture the bogeyman coming at you in four different Halloween costumes. The first is as an enemy,
someone hatefully devoted to your psychological
destruction. Your assignment is to love him. That
means actively contribute to his well-being. Invest
your time, effort, comfort, and possessions in
benefiting him.

The second costume is that of a persecutor. Greet
him with a prayer for his long life and happiness. "Pray
for those who persecute you" does not mean to ask
God to make your life easier by changing them. It does
not mean, "Dear God, here's this rotten persecutor
again. Please shape him up. Oh, convince him of how
mean and inconsiderate he has been to me. Show him
the error of his ways and relieve me of having to
defend myself against his embarrassing attacks."

Instead, pray with the mind of Jesus, who came to
give even bad guys abundant life. "Father of both of us,
I am speaking to You on behalf of this person whom
You have brought into my life. Lavish Your abundant
riches upon him. Prosper him, thrill him to the

deepest core of his being. Relieve him of guilt and hate and fear and loneliness. Convince him he is precious to You. Thank You for the privilege of calling him my friend."

The third time the bogeyman trick-or-treater knocks on your door, he is blaring curses at you out of portable stereo speakers he carries. Your disciple's manual instructs you to bless him. You do that first with your face. You beam a giant grin at him. Then you tell him you are especially glad to see him, because you have some good thoughts you eagerly want to wish upon him. Go on to say you confer upon him God's favor. Bid him long life and prosperity and success and contentment and good health and many friends. If he would not be offended by it, extend your hand and place it on his shoulder or head or cheek as you smile and pronounce these blessings.

On his fourth visit, the bogeyman comes garbed as an exploiter who despitefully uses you. To him, do good. Give him something that belongs to you that you think might inwardly thrill him, whether he ever shows it outwardly or not. Show hospitality. Offer him a cup of coffee that you fix with your own hands. Better yet a whole meal, without any lesson-teaching conversation from you.

Speak well of him to others. Polish his reputation. Tell him the strong positive character traits you see in him. Encourage him. Give him your vote of confidence. Trust him with something that matters to you, that you're fairly sure he is able to handle. If he blows it, calmly say you are sorry it turned out that way, and that you two can try it again another time.

Why do these four things? To shock some sense into these bad actors? To pile up credits with Christ so He'll excuse you from rougher duty elsewhere? No, strictly to stretch. God gave you muscles of courage. *Take* courage by stretching those muscles deliberately in directions they do not spontaneously want to go.

We have misplaced our fears. We have shown greater awe for our bogeymen than for God. He alone is worthy of our fear. He alone controls our heartbeat, our fragile planet's integrity, and our eternal destiny. We are in His hands, whether we like it or not.

Think of yourself as a frightened non-swimmer clinging desperately to a life raft in the Pacific Ocean. It is your security and you refuse to leave it, even to board the luxury liner that has just pulled up alongside you. But may Captain Jesus have your permission to hoist you, in your raft, into the swimming pool aboard the ship?

Several decades after Jesus walked on the water of a stormy Sea of Galilee, an eyewitness calmly retold the story. That writer quoted Christ's emphatic antidote for fear: "It is I; be not afraid! — I AM; stop being frightened!" (John 6:20, Amplified).

We can define fear as emotional energy available to get information about unfamiliar situations we cannot avoid. Jesus responded to that information hunger in His frightened disciples, by offering the fundamental fact that makes everything else make sense: "I AM." It was Jehovah's declaration of being to Moses (Exodus 3:14). It is the reason Christ offers us to fear not in any situation.

God exists! More than that, God personally declares to us for our relief and benefit that He exists and that He rules. He will use His power over us to caress and heal and nourish and cuddle and comfort. We are secure only in those magnificent hands that could crush us, for they belong to Jesus, who stared the bogeyman in the face through Good Friday, then put him in the grave on Easter.

CHAPTER TWELVE

The Choice Is Ours

*I*t is reasonable to assume that Jesus entered manhood with some aspects of His childhood still undisciplined. Like us, He had lived with imperfect parents who must have made mistakes. Yet history does not portray Him as a strong-willed adult — childish, stubborn, self-centered. What happened between the time He stopped being under the imperfect authority and discipline of His parents, and the time He entered His public ministry consistently under the authority of the God Whom He called "Father"?

From the story of Jesus in the temple, at the end of Luke, chapter 2, we skip to the start of Luke, chapter 4, where we have the story of His temptation in the desert. It was that same rocky, barren, dusty, hot, scorpion-infested country that groomed John the Baptist into an effective tool in God's hands. Jesus was out there voluntarily, in response to the leading of the Holy Spirit. He did not eat. He was hungry, under stress.

Beliefs, our deepest guiding principles for life, show most plainly under stress. Psychologically we say that under stress we regress. That is, we fall back on coping mechanisms we developed in early childhood years. We're all familiar with the kinds of childish things we do when the usual, polite, cooperative ways seem not to get us what we want. We resort to tantrums, pouting, whining, and being helpless in order to force somebody else to do for us what we ought to do for ourselves. We fall back on immature, strong-willed child maneuvers.

Here was Jesus, deliberately putting Himself into a situation where He would be tempted to resort to immature ways. I think He deliberately did what we must all do in one way or another in order to become mature. We must consciously choose, by an act of will, what our guidelines for living are going to be, and whose authority we will respect as ultimate.

The strong-willed part of us that is still undisciplined acknowledges no higher authority than self. The 1970's were called the "me" generation, and the movement is still a fad. It says, "You've got to love, think about, and value yourself first if you're going to be able to love other people."

That's backwards!

Our inclination as kids is to think we are the center of the universe, that nothing is more magnificent than we. Each of us tends to think, "If I am helpless, you are duty-bound to step in and do something for me." We insist that our woes and our wants must become the most important considerations in other people's lives. As kids, we all have this kind of arrogance. The hallmark of maturity is our turning outward in loving concern for the well-being of others.

Egocentricity is normal in our early stages of intellectual development. It has been well described by the Swiss psychologist, Piaget. Each child is kind of a budding scientist, coming up with explanations for why things are the way they are. For example, a child who is asked why it gets dark at night will answer, "To make me go to bed." The child's theory is, "Everything is arranged around and for me."

It's not a bad guess; it fits a lot of the facts. Especially with a first-born child (which Jesus was), every burp is a big deal to the parents. The child mumbles "da-da" and the parents think they have an orator in the house. For us to think the world revolves around us is a universal stage of human development. Under stress later in life, we tend to regress and fall back upon this as a working hypothesis to make sense of what is happening to us, and to guide our actions. At this point of vulnerability, Satan mounts a major effort to contaminate God's creation. He is not able to keep us from being made in the image of God. That's beyond his ability. God beat him to the punch. We *are* made in the image of God. So, the best that Satan can do is spitefully try to mar that image. He cannot keep us from being creative, but if he can sidetrack the way we use our creativity, he gets some satisfaction. He is the original rebel. He cannot keep us from being children of God, but he seeks to keep us from becoming adults of God. He seeks to keep us bound up in childish thinking, for it is in the realm of our thinking that Satan works. That is where we wrestle — not against flesh and blood, but against principalities, against powers, against spiritual wickedness in heavenly places (Ephesians 6:12).

The struggle is in our minds. That's where it was with Jesus. We are to be transformed by the renewing of our minds (Romans 12:2). He heard, at least as strongly as you and I have ever heard or sensed or felt, the tempting voice. Its first appeal: "You're hungry, right? Well, I'll tell You what," Satan said. "Let the primary guideline for Your life be physical comfort."

Did it ever strike you, in thinking about this story of Jesus in the desert, that the people who wrote about it weren't there? The only witness to those events was Jesus Himself. He was the original teller of this story. So, what we have, in Matthew 4 and Luke 4, is a story summarized in the way Jesus considered most significant. He said in one way or another to His disciples, "Of all the struggles I went through out there for forty days, three were important. My philosophy of life boiled down to three key principles. The first temptation was to make physical comfort a primary goal of My life, to make it an idol, something I *needed*."

The devil approached Jesus on the basis of His identity. He said, "*If* You are the Son of God, command these stones to turn into bread." Brilliant strategy on Satan's part. He realized that part of what Jesus was doing out there in the wilderness was working out His identity. In later years He was to ask His followers, "Whom do men say I am? Whom do you say I am?" In the wilderness He was answering the question, "Whom do *I* say I am?"

Psychology teaches that one of the final tasks we all face in the transition from childhood to adult maturity is that of solving the identity crisis. Jesus had been taught by His parents that He was the Son of God in a special way. But how could He *know* He was? At what point in His life must He have made the decision to accept that identity and live by it?

He may have had to struggle through it and work it out while He was in the desert. Satan had a vested interest in sidetracking Him. So he insinuated maybe Jesus wasn't the Son of God: "*If* You are, then use Your power for Your comfort. You're hungry. You deserve a break today, don't You?"

Jesus wisely did not play into Satan's hands. If He had taken offense at the insinuation, He'd have said indignantly, "What do you mean 'If'? I'll show you! There, zap, some bread." If Jesus had produced the bread, He would have been following orders from Satan. In trying to show Satan who's boss, He would have unwittingly allowed Satan to be boss. Instead, He stuck to the issue: Will comfort be My priority?

Jesus answered, "It is written, 'Man shall not live by bread alone, but by every word that proceeds out of the mouth of God.'" He took His stand. Not once, but three times. Each time He chose an explicit standard for conducting His life. Each time His standard was the written Scriptures of the Hebrew religion. All three quotations were from Deuteronomy.

Jesus chose consciously to abdicate Himself as highest authority in His own life, thus leaving behind Him the ways of childhood. He deliberately chose that the authority in His adult life would be the written Word of God. And so He said, "OK, rather than live primarily for My own comfort, I will live by the Word of God." And the bread He was hungry for symbolized the physical comforts that we all hunger for: warmth, money and the luxuries it can buy, and relief from pain.

At times when I've been in pain, I have thought I would do anything just to be free from it. I used to get car-sick as a kid. I hated it. And I believe if the devil had appeared, even in horns and red costume, and made me an offer, I would have gladly said, "You can burn my soul in hell forever if you'll just get me over this nausea right now."

But Jesus said that a higher priority for Him was to be intimate with the God of the universe, the personal source of all reality.

Then Satan came at Him a second way. From a lofty spire of the temple, he suggested Jesus throw Himself down. Here, he was appealing to a common wish we all entertain, to be free from the natural consequences of our own foolish actions. I would like to read a book while driving down the highway at full speed. With that desire there is also the thought in me that I ought to be allowed to do that. The laws of the universe should bend themselves to accommodate me. The way I think can be put like this: "*If* God loves me (notice the "if" of doubt, rather than the "since" of faith), He'll keep me from being hurt. I am entitled to do what I want to do." There is something in us that

wants to be free to do what we want to do and not
experience the lawful natural consequences. We want
to be above laws. Hence, above the Lawmaker. We
would be higher than the Most High.

Satan dangled that little morsel in front of Jesus.
Jesus answered, "It is written, 'You shall not tempt, or
try, or test exceedingly the Lord your God.'" He
decided He would not engage in foolish actions, ex-
pecting God to come and rescue Him. That's a way of
twisting God's arm. It's blackmail. "Hey, God, here's
an offer You can't refuse. Either spare Me or have Your
reputation smudged."

People — especially superstitious Christians —
often do that at major decision points in their lives,
like getting married. The approach is something like
this: "Well, I think I ought to marry so-and-so, and if
God doesn't want me to, He'll stop me." In a way this
implies that, if God is going to avoid being embarrassed, He'll have to come through with what I
want. We try to back God into a corner.

Suppose Jesus had thrown Himself off the temple.
On the way down, He'd be daring God: "Now, if You
want the gospel preached in Galilee, in Jerusalem,
Judea, Samaria, and the uttermost parts of the earth,
You're gonna have to cushion me before I hit that hard
ground." It's a way of acting as if I can take power over
God. It's a childish effort to make Him bend to my
strong will.

But Jesus declared, "God does not deal that way. It
is written, 'Thou shalt not push the Lord thy God into
a corner.'" That's a liberal translation, but it's the idea.

The third temptation Satan tried on Jesus summarized the other two. He showed Jesus in a glimpse
all the political power, control and influence in the
world, all the real estate He could control, all the
kingdoms and possessions. Jesus could have
everything and everyone under His orders. That is

certainly appealing. Think of all the good He could do. He could stop the abuse of power by the Romans. He could legislate morality, eliminate poverty, institute justice. Satan said, "I'll give You all this if You'll just do one small, simple thing — just worship me, just once."

When we do not acknowledge God as the highest authority in our lives, by default our highest authority is ourselves. However, that's not precisely true, because we are not the initiators of the conspiracy of opposition against God's authority.

In reality, we become followers of a movement already under way, initiated long ago and still captained by Satan. It is the only alternative to agreeing with God's right to rule. When we think we are making our own, independent decisions, we are just going along with the propaganda, the sales pitch of an advertising campaign. There's no originality in deciding to rebel against God.

That's where Satan makes his move into our lives, by contaminating our thinking, to have us live under the illusion that we are the center of our lives, when really he is the one in control. The temptation Jesus faced, was to go His own way. Giving in to that temptation is what it means to worship Satan.

At the end of the book of Judges there is a pithy sentence which says that after all the leaders and judges had run their course, there was no king in Israel (no leader, no acknowledged authority), "... and every man did what was right in his own eyes." The result of that was anarchy and chaos. People were authorities to themselves. Satan was in control. God was still revered as kind of a sham, as the nominal god of the Jews. But there was no heart worship, because there was no explicit choosing of an external authority, such as Jesus chose.

Jesus said, "Be gone Satan, leave Me, for it is

written, 'You shall do homage to and worship only the Lord your God, and Him only shall you serve.'"

Jesus' choice was 180°, directly opposite, from the choice Adam and his wife made at the first fork in the road for mankind, the first test of allegiance. They liked the idea that they could have power through the knowledge of good and evil. "You can be like God." That was the offer Satan made to the man and woman, our representatives. It has a drunken appeal to us. Be like God? Wow! You mean invulnerable? I could have what I want when I want it? I would not even have to depend on God for comfort, for food, for security? I could be permanently secure? Permanently powerful?

There is something in us that lusts for power — power that will insure we never again feel inadequate, power that will insulate us from ever feeling inferior in any way. We long to be superior to every other power.

And to that appeal, Jesus said, "No. I will not make the decision that Adam and Eve did. I will make a different decision. I am the image of God and He is Number One. He is in control. And the best that I know of Him and His wishes for Me are what are recorded in the written Scriptures of the Jewish religion."

We, as followers of Christ, do well to imitate His example and choose as the explicit authority in our lives the written Scriptures of the Old and New Testaments. Our Master has demonstrated for us this alternative to living frustrated lives as strong-willed adults.

God's majesty was revealed in the bold, courageous decisions Jesus made those three times when He said, "No. The Lord is King. He is in charge. He is the only one worthy of the loyalty of our lives."

It is when we make those same choices that we can say with Paul, "When I was a [strong-willed] child, I used to speak as a [strong-willed] child, think as a [strong-willed] child, reason as a [strong-willed] child; when I became a man, I did away with childish things. For now we see in a mirror dimly, but then face to face; now I know in part, but then I shall know fully just as I also have been fully known" (1 Corinthians 13:11-12,NASB). "Brethren, I do not regard myself as having laid hold of it yet; but one thing I do: forgetting what lies behind and reaching forward to what lies ahead, I press on toward the goal for the prize of the upward call of God in Christ Jesus. Let us therefore, as many as are perfect [adult, mature], have this attitude" (Philippians 3:13-15a, NASB).

BIBLIOGRAPHY

Berne, Eric. *Games People Play*. New
York: Grove Press, 1964.

Buber, Martin. *I And Thou* (2nd ed.). New
York: Charles Scribner's Sons, 1958.

Chambers, Oswald. *My Utmost for His Highest*.
New York: Dodd, Mead & Company, 1935.

Dobson, James. *The Strong-Willed Child*.
Wheaton, IL: Tyndale, 1978.

Dreikurs, Rudolf and Soltz, Vicki. *Children: The
Challenge*. New York: Hawthorn Books,
1964.

Gothard, Bill. *Ninth Annual National Advanced
Seminar* (Indiana University, August,
1977). Oak Brook, IL: Institute in Basic Youth
Conflicts.

Harris, Thomas A. *I'm OK-You're OK*. New
York: Harper and Row, 1969.

Horney, Karen. *Neurosis and Human Growth*.
New York: Norton, 1950.

James, Muriel and Jongeward, Dorothy. *Born to
Win*. Reading, MA: Addison-Wesley, 1971.

Keller, Philip. *A Shepherd Looks at Psalm 23*.
Grand Rapids, MI: Zondervan, 1970.

Phillips, John B. *Your God Is Too Small*.
London: Epworth Press, 1952.

Smith, Hannah Whitall. *The Christian's Secret of
a Happy Life*. Westwood, NJ: Revell,
1952.

Souter, Alexander, ed. *Pocket Lexicon of the
Greek New Testament*. New York: Oxford
University Press, 1916.

Stapleton, Ruth Carter. *The Gift of Inner Healing.* Waco, Texas: Word Books, 1976.
Taylor, Dr. & Mrs. Howard. *Hudson Taylor's Spiritual Secret.* Chicago: Moody Press, 1932.